ENERGY
POWER
SHIFT

"An informed democracy will behave in a responsible fashion".
Thomas Jefferson

ENERGY
POWER
SHIFT

BARRY J. HANSON

Lakota Scientific Press
Maple, Wisconsin

Special thank you to Dr. Jack Zaengle for help and encouragement

Additional copies of this book are available for bulk pur-
chases. For more information, please contact: Lakota
Scientific Press, 3194 South Smith Creek Road, Maple
Wisconsin 54854 or call
715-372-5161 fax: 715-372-5105
Internet access: www.energypowershift.com

ISBN:0-9758500-0-8

Dedicated to our daughter
Heidi

CONTENTS

Introduction 8

CHAPTER I   BREAKTHROUGH TECHNOLOGIES 15

The Major Players 16
The Thermal Conversion Process (TCP) 16
Waste and Biomass to Oil
The Large Plug in Diesel Hybrid Electric Vehicle (PDHEV) 20
Hydraulic Drive 32
New Battery Technologies 33
Lithium-ion, Lithium Sulfur, Polymer Based Rechargeable Alkaline
Hydrogen Fuel Cell Vehicle Compared to the PDHEV 30
Fuel Cells 33
Sun to Heat Technologies 40
Solar Thermal, Passive Solar, Ground Mounted Solar Systems
New Developments in Photovoltaics 43
New Developments in Wind Generation 47
Ocean Systems 51
Wave Energy Conversion, Underwater Turbines
More Ways to Produce Clean Liquid Fuels 54
Methanol Synthesis, Ethylene Synthesis, Fischer-Tropsch Chemistry, Mobil-M, Fast Pyrolysis

CHAPTER 2   BASIC ENERGY CONCEPTS 61
Primary Energy and End Use Energy 62
Where Energy is Found 65
Wind 71
Ocean Waves and Currents 73
The Conversion of Primary Energy to Useful Forms 74
Conservation and Efficiency 77
Distributed Generation 77
Some Hydrogen Physics 79
Related Concepts 81
Sustainability, Capital and Income, Sustainable Growth, The Commons,
Exponential Growth, Externalities, Global Warming Basics

CHAPTER 3   THE OLD WAY OF ACQUIRING ENERGY 93
Electricity from Coal 94
Electricity from Nuclear 103
Gasoline from Foreign Oil 113

CHAPTER 4   HOW MUCH ENERGY DO WE NEED? 125
Transportation 125
Space Heat and Domestic Hot Water 127
Electricity 129

CHAPTER 5   HOW MUCH ENERGY DO WE HAVE? · 133

Waste and Biomass · 134

Annual Waste and Biomass Resources for the U.S. Chart · · · · · · · · · · · · · · 135

Wind · 136

The Sun · 141

Other Renewable Energy Resources · 142

Offshore Wind · 142

Geothermal · 143

CHAPTER 6   ECONOMIC STRATEGIES · 147

TCP Plant Economic Analysis · 150

High Temperature Fuel Cell Economic Analysis · 152

Fuel Cell Energy Flow Chart · 155

Wind Energy Economic Analysis · 156

Adding Value to 138 Pounds of Waste · 158

An Economic Strategy for a Typical County · 160

An Economic Strategy for America · 163

Powering Southern California on Seaweed · 169

Cross-Country on Restaurant Grease · 170

Buying Wind Energy From the Good Citizens of
North and South Dakota · 172

Cows into Oil · 173

CHAPTER 7   A MATTER OF CHOICE · 175

If You Could Choose · 177
Funding The Renewable Energy Economy

Too Costly? Too Impractical? Evaluation Charts · 185

Handy Checklist · 188
Comparing Strategies for Acquiring Liquid Fuels, Comparing Strategies for Producing Electricity

Conclusion · 191

What You Can Do · 192

Bibliography · 197

Internet Resources · 197

Oil Terminology · 199

Index · 200

INTRODUCTION

There is a myth being perpetuated that transitioning from our current fossil fuel and nuclear based economy to one based entirely on clean, renewable energy would be "too costly" and "impractical." This book was written to dispel that myth.

The fact of the matter is that the U.S. has five times more clean energy than it needs to deliver all energy services. New technologies that were not available only a few years ago are either now ready to be put into use or are very close to commercialization.

A renewable energy based economy would save the U.S. $750 billion per year plus create over six million new jobs which would revitalize local communities all across the country. A renewable energy based economy would reduce the federal trade deficit, enhance national security and essentially solve a staggering array of environmental problems. A renewable energy based economy would require LESS government, less taxation, less spending, less welfare and less regulation fostering an atmosphere that allows a free market economy to flourish.

Two new patented processes now make it possible to transform sewage, plastics, used tires, forestry waste, agricultural waste, animal carcasses and biomass into oil. That's right...oil, the stuff we go half way around the world and dedicate a huge percentage of our national resources to secure. We have enough waste and available biomass in the U.S. to make one hundred billion gallons of oil per year. That is enough oil for all of our transportation needs and more.

This oil, now made in local communities all across the country, can also be used to fire high temperature fuel cells. Newly developed "thin film solid oxide" fuel cells operate quietly, cleanly, efficiently and inexpensively generating both electricity and heat on site where it will be used. There is no longer a need for an electrical grid or a utility company for that matter.

A new breed of SUV-sized diesel hybrid electric vehicles, utilizing new battery technologies coupled with small diesel engines, hydraulic drives and powerful electric motors now part of the wheel itself, run the entire year on seventy gallons of the oil...single-handedly eliminating the federal trade deficit for foreign oil. The U.S. transportation fuel demand will be cut from 140 billion gallons per year to 10 billion gallons of clean non-fossil oil.

New technologies now make it possible to tap into the tremendous kinetic energy of the Gulf Stream to make electricity or to harness the energy of ocean waves -- energy there for the taking by those with enough imagination and entrepreneurial spirit to capture it and sell it.

Nanotechnology, a whole new world of devices created on a molecular scale, is finding its way into energy applications with dye sensitized solar collectors on thin films of flexible plastic that make electricity directly from the sun. These continuous sheets of energy producing plastic film can be used as roofing or applied directly to the building skin; it can even be made into clothing or built into the rooftop of hybrid vehicles.

This is the "new way" of acquiring energy contrasted with the "old way"…the way it is done now with an economy that runs on very dirty coal, oil from half way around the world and a nuclear industry that must rely on the taxpayer to pay for their potential liabilities because there is no insurance company that will do it. While this old way of doing things may work just fine for a handful of politically connected utilities and some multinational oil companies, it is not working so well for the average American, nor does it bode well for future generations.

The renewable energy approach carries with it some distinct economic advantages…in fact they add up to over $750 billion per year. The primary energy is free, for the most part, in the form of waste, biomass, wind, sun and ocean movement. In addition to the primary energy being free, it is converted to useful energy with much greater efficiency and with much less waste than with current methods. Electricity now costs more to deliver than to generate, and it is only generated at a 35% efficiency. With renewable energy, there are no clean up costs…no surface mine reclamation, no toxic piles of contaminated ore next to pristine rivers and no mercury emissions into the air. There will be no more need to subsidize mature, highly profitable, polluting industries which now cost the taxpayer billions of dollars a year. With renewable energy, the trade deficit would be reduced by a third, overnight, by eliminating the $200 billion a year we currently send overseas for oil alone. With renewable energy, there is no need for military involvement in the acquisition of oil and the protection for corporations to have access to oil at a cost of over $100 billion in taxpayer expense.

The renewable energy approach carries with it some distinct social benefits as well. Millions of new, high paying jobs that cannot be shipped overseas would be created, contributing to the revitalization of communities all across the country. The renewable energy approach provides for greater national security eliminating vulnerable targets. Consider not having to worry about 1000 foot long LNG tankers sitting in ports, each one with the equivalent concentrated energy of forty Hiroshima atomic bombs and knowing that a couple of bazooka rounds could set it off. Consider our already trouble prone electrical grid that depends on thousands of computer interfaced control points that could be hacked into by a terrorist group...bringing the system to its knees. Consider the hundreds of thousands of exposed oil and gas pipelines where two people on a weekend in the right places in Louisiana could shut off the gas to the entire Eastern seaboard. Consider, too, the hundred or so nuclear plants with their vulnerabilities to sabotage, their record of accidents and the lackluster oversight of their operation and safety.

Probably the most significant social benefit that a renewable approach would bring is relative to the environment. From global warming to acid rain and nuclear waste, a whole host of environmental nightmares would be eliminated at their source.

A renewable energy economy should not be confused with the much touted "hydrogen economy." A renewable energy economy is ready to go...now.

The choice is really quite simple, we can choose to purchase our energy from Saudi princes....or North Dakota farmers.

THE OLD WAY

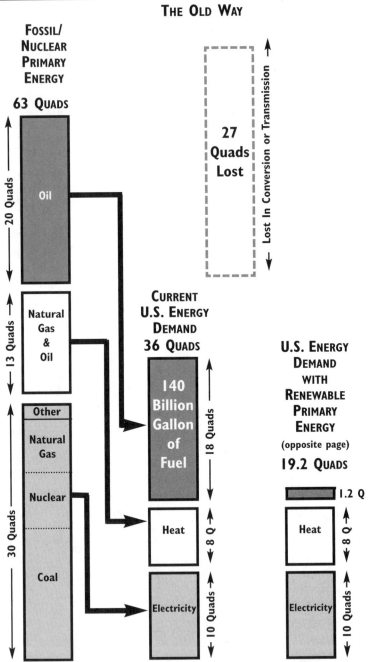

The above illustration contrasts the old way of supplying the current U.S. energy demand with the new way which utilizes renewable primary energy and new technologies to provide equivalent energy services while reducing demand from 36 Quads to 19.2 Quads. One Quad = 10^{15} BTUs

THE NEW WAY

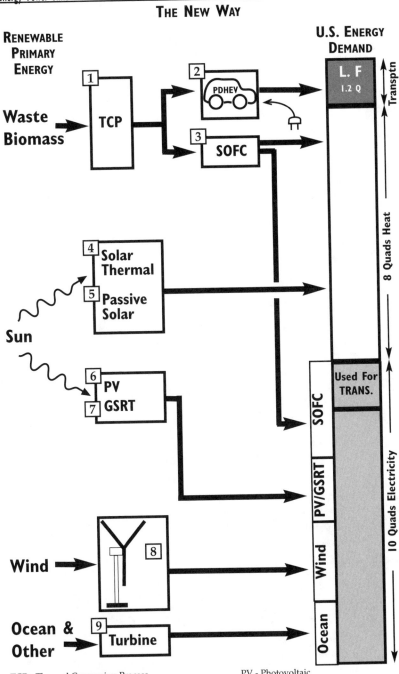

TCP - Thermal Conversion Process
PDHEV - Plug In Diesel Hybrid Electric Vehicle
GSRT - Ground Contact Solar w/Refrigerant Turbine

PV - Photovoltaic
SOFC - Solid Oxide Fuel Cell
LF - Liquid Fuel

 # Breakthrough Technologies

EMERGING TECHNOLOGIES

Currently, we are in a world wide, technological revolution that promises to dramatically change the way we acquire and use energy. What was impossible just a few years ago is quite possible today:

- turn garbage into oil -- sewage sludge, plastics, used tires, dead livestock, even toxic waste -- for 40 cents per gallon...in your own community creating thousands of jobs and improving the environment at the same time

- drive a full-sized SUV for a year on just 70 gallons of fuel

- generate electricity from a suitcase-sized fuel cell that's reliable, silent, and clean with free heat and hot water to boot ...no more utility bills.

- generate electricity from roofing material that converts sunlight directly into electricity using special dyes and nanotechnology, or take advantage of the enormous kinetic energy of the Gulf Stream to make inexpensive electricity.

These exciting new breakthrough technologies make transitioning to a renewable energy economy a practical reality unforeseen even a few short years ago. Most of the technologies described here are commercially available today; the others are on the brink of commercialization.

The transition made possible by these breakthrough technologies will have far reaching political, social and economic implications -- creating millions of jobs, revitalizing local economies, reducing the federal trade deficit, enhancing national security and improving the environment.

THE MAJOR PLAYERS

Four new technologies dominate the renewable energy horizon because together, they have the potential to transform the way we acquire and use energy. Far from being "too costly," these emerging technologies will pay for themselves.

- Thermal conversion process (TCP)
- Large, plug-in diesel hybrid electric vehicle (PDHEV)
- The high temperature fuel cell
- Ocean current and wave energy conversion systems

In addition to the new technologies, innovations in photovoltaics and the commercial success of mature industries such as wind round out the components of the renewable energy economy. The result is a dramatic look at the old ways of acquiring energy compared to this new way to tap free energy from wind, sun and waste.

THERMAL CONVERSION PROCESS (TCP)

Thermal Conversion[1] is a closed process, whereby a large variety of feedstock can be converted to a light #2 fuel oil and other by-products, such as carbon, sterilized water and fertilizer grade minerals. Since there are no emissions to the environment, the plant is permitted as a manufacturing process and not a waste treatment or waste disposal process. There is currently one commercial scale (200 tons per day) plant in operation in Missouri, one pilot plant (7 tons per day) in Pennsylvania and plants in various stages of completion in Alabama, Nevada, Colorado and Italy.

TCP promises to eliminate the need for communities to incinerate or landfill waste by instead converting waste streams into high quality lightweight oil, as well as other valuable by-products. The plant mimics the geological processes of high pressure and temperature that, over millions of years, converted organic matter into crude oil deep below the surface of the earth. The main difference is that it does it very quickly. Almost any organic material, under the right conditions, can be made to depolymerize by breaking down the long chain molecules into atoms and much smaller molecules. Once broken down completely, they can be reassembled into oil with by-products consisting of sterilized minerals, combustible gases (used in the process itself for heat),

---

[1]Lemley, Brad. "Anything into Oil," Discover Magazine. May 2003.
<www.discover.com/may_03/featoil.html>

carbon black and water. One secret of the process is that it does not attempt to drive off the water contained in the waste stream, which is an energy inefficient process. Instead, it uses the water in the waste to facilitate the thermal conversion process itself.

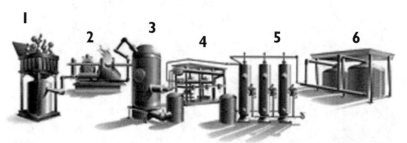

FIGURE 1.1 The TCP diagram. (1) Slurring the organic and inorganic feed with water. (2) Heating the slurry under pressure to reaction temperature. (3) Flashing the slurry to a lower pressure to release the gaseous products after the initial reaction is complete. (4) Reformer reactor segments solids from volatile chemicals. (5) Heating the oil to drive off water and to separate the light oils from gases. (6) Separation and storage of the light oils and gases. Diagram courtesy of Changing World Technologies, Inc.

Potentially toxic material, such as PVC (polyvinyl chloride) plastic, can be safely dealt with by using TCP. If incinerated, PVC produces deadly dioxin, but with thermal conversion PVC is depolymerized to produce oil and hydrochloric acid, a useful by-product. Hospital waste, diseased cattle, feedlot manure, paper, yard waste, agricultural crop waste, forestry waste, cardboard, plastics, used tires, municipal solid waste, garbage, sewage sludge, even anthrax, could be safely and economically depolymerized and reconstituted into oil and other nontoxic, useful products.

Pyrolysis, and other methods of converting waste into useful materials, especially oil, have been tried in the past with little success because the cost was too great and the quality of the oil was poor. The developers of the patented TC-type process have now apparently solved these operational and engineering problems (see also fast pyrolysis page 60).

There is usually a tipping fee for approximately half of the waste/biomass tonnage. The tipping fees for municipal solid waste are now ranging to well above $100 per ton in some parts of the country; the fees to dispose of hazardous material can be thousands of dollars per ton.

FIGURE 1.2 A two hundred ton per day TCP plant at Carthage, Missouri is now selling oil commercially. By the end of 2004, this plant will be selling 21,000 gallons per day. Photo courtesy of Changing World Technologies

Material that was formerly an expensive liability and an environmental nightmare in some cases, is now an asset worth at least $50 per ton. Hazardous chemicals are depolymerized into valuable minerals and oil. Feedstock, such as biomass and forestry waste, could be paid for by the plant at a rate of about $50 per ton with money collected in fees for the other material.

Plastics would not have to be separated out of the waste stream for processing in the TCP plant. In fact, landfills and recycling would become obsolete. Illegal hazardous dumping would become a problem of the past because now the hazardous material itself has value as feedstock for the TC process.

The components are off the shelf, but the engineering required to build a commercial scale plant is specialized and proprietary to one development firm, Changing World Technologies of Hempstead, New York. It will take this company about three or four years to train a technical staff to oversee the licensing of this technology, at which time their plans are to license the construction of numerous 1000 ton per day plants throughout the U.S. and possibly overseas as well. Currently, they have five commercial plants in various stages of permitting and construction -- most of the engineering troubleshooting has already been accomplished at the Carthage, Missouri plant.

A huge variety of feedstock -- including cellulosic biomass, paper products, wood, lignin and various carbohydrates, including the accompanying water -- can be macerated and converted into a high quality fuel oil. In other words, the process is not dependent on lipids and high molecular weight hydrocarbons or organic fats as feedstock, where the requirement would simply be to break them down into shorter chain hydrocarbons.

The process is proving to be between 80 and 90% efficient depending on the feedstock, and it requires no outside energy input. About one third of the product is syn-gas, which is fed back into the system to fuel it; there are no emissions to the environment.[2]

It would be hard to find a more attractive economic strategy than being able to convert waste, much less toxic waste, into a valuable, energy dense liquid fuel. TCP plants could be built literally on the landfill site and the accumulated wastes used in the process.

This process has the potential to produce over 100 billion gallons of oil per year from waste and biomass, virtually eliminating the need for foreign oil.

In addition to oil, the TC process produces 60 pounds of fertilizer grade minerals per ton of feedstock, and up to 700 pounds of carbon black and distilled water. The carbon is worth up to $1 per pound after activation, which means that the carbon has more economic value than the oil, and it was not even included in the payback calculations.

The installed cost for a 1000-ton per day plant is $65 million. The plant in Missouri was projected to cost under $20 million, but it came in somewhat higher than that because, as the first full-scale plant, there were additional start up expenses. The components will become standardized as more plants are installed and the cost should come down.

The cost to produce oil with the TC process is about 40 cents per gallon, 28 cents in operation and maintenance and 12 cents financing and capitol costs over ten years. The production cost of the oil is expected to come down to around 20 cents per gallon as more plants come online.

---

[2]Telephone interview with Changing World Technologies CEO Brian Appel, April 2004.

A 1000-ton per day plant requires 100 permanent full time employees to run it and 600 construction jobs to build it. Feedstock is purchased from the local community, and the products from the plant are marketed within the local economy. Purchasing biomass from local farmers at $50 per ton puts $20 billion per year into the households of family farms across the country.

There is enough available waste and biomass in the U.S. to accommodate a plant in every county in America, which in turn would sell $30 million worth of oil per year to local citizens in every county.

All liquid fuel for the U.S. demand would be produced within the country avoiding a $200 billion per year trade deficit. This strategy alone would eliminate the perceived need to acquire foreign oil.

With this strategy fully implemented, there would be no need for recycling, toxic waste would no longer be a disposal problem, landfills and incineration would become obsolete, thereby reducing environmental problems. It is known that the TC process destroys the mad cow disease (Bovine spongeform encephalopathy) prion. The oil itself is carbon neutral and does not contain sulfur, as does fossil diesel fuel.

THE LARGE PLUG IN DIESEL HYBRID ELECTRIC VEHICLE (PDHEV)

As the term suggests, a hybrid combines two operational systems which work together (see Figure 1.3). In the case of transportation technologies, the hybrid uses two motors and two fuels. An example of this is the railroad locomotive which is a diesel/electric hybrid. The diesel engine does not directly power the locomotive; the diesel powers a generator that makes electricity which powers the electric motors that drive the wheels.

The first hydrogen fuel cell powered locomotive has already been tested. The 109-ton locomotive uses a one megawatt fuel cell to supply the electricity for electric motors at each wheel. The architecture of the locomotive remains the same, with electric drive for the propulsion where the fuel cell has simply replaced the diesel engine/generator combination.

The cruise ship Queen Mary-2 is another example of a diesel/electric hybrid which uses 85 megawatt (157,000 horse power) electric motors to drive the props. They are fed electricity from generators driven by diesel engines.

Figure 1.3

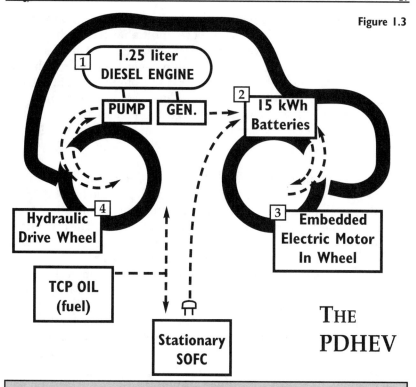

1.25 liter DIESEL ENGINE

PUMP **GEN.**

15 kWh Batteries

Hydraulic Drive Wheel

Embedded Electric Motor In Wheel

TCP OIL (fuel)

Stationary SOFC

THE
PDHEV

1. A small displacement diesel engine drives a hydraulic pump and an electric generator. Notice that there is NO drive train, NO transmission, NO differential and NO axles. The hydraulic drive replaces the traditional drive train. The diesel engine uses #2 fuel oil from the TCP plant as fuel, as does the stationary solid oxide fuel cell (SOFC).

2. The onboard battery pack, which drives the front wheels, stores 15 kWh of electricity -- enough to cover 60 miles without recharging. The battery pack is recharged three ways: regenerative braking while underway, by turning on the diesel engine while underway, and by plugging into a stationary power source while parked. It could be charged a fourth way also, with polymer solar cells built into the roof of the vehicle. This battery pack weighs about 160 pounds; comparable capacity lead-acid batteries would weigh about 900 pounds, five times as much.

3. The front wheels contain 35 KW embedded electric motors and provide instantaneous torque at low speeds and instant acceleration at low or high way speeds. Upon braking, the electric motor becomes a generator, putting energy back into the batteries.

4. Hydraulic fluid pressure drives the rear wheels. A regenerative braking system stores energy in a nitrogen gas accumulator when the rear brakes are applied. Upon acceleration, the energy is directed back to the wheel.

Diesel hybrids are more efficient, cleaner and have performance bene-fits over straight diesel power in those applications, and the hybrid principle works just as well for cars, SUVs and light trucks. The PDHEV is featured as a significant technological breakthrough that allows for a reduction of liquid fuel demand from the current 140 bil-lion gallons per year to 10 billion gallons per year. There is a need for electricity (660 billion kWh) to recharge the battery portion of the hybrid, but it is much easier to provide clean electricity than it is to acquire foreign oil.

The hybrid automobile or light truck also uses two motors and two dif-ferent fuels to accommodate two distinctly different modes of driving. One driving mode has the vehicle starting, stopping, accelerating, brak-ing and at times requiring plenty of torque or traction. The other driv-ing mode has the vehicle cruising as efficiently as possible -- speeding along at a constant 70 mph for hours at a time. Attempting to do both with one engine is inefficient and compromises optimum performance in both driving modes.

So, why not have a separate power plant for each driving mode that is optimal for that cycle? The hybrid does just that. This is how efficien-cies of over 60 mpg of liquid fuel can be achieved in a full sized SUV type vehicle.

Hybrid Features

The Embedded Electric Motor

For the torque, acceleration and quick power in stop and go driving, the Hybrid Electric Vehicle (HEV) uses an electric motor which goes from zero to maximum torque instantaneously.[3] Instead of mounting the electric motor and then using a drive connected with a drive train to the wheels, the HEV transforms the wheel itself into a 95% efficient electric motor (see Figure 1.4). Several companies, such as Wavecrest Laboratories, General Motors and UQM Technologies, are developing this breakthrough -- the technology of the "embedded electric motor." Power is now delivered to the wheel with a wire instead of an ineffi-cient, heavy and expensive mechanical drive train. Not only that, but the power to the wheel is controlled much better than with a drive train; electronic sensors at each wheel tell the controller exactly how much traction is needed at that wheel.

---

[3] For example, the Dodge Ram pickup truck advertises 600 lb-ft of torque. The performance data from Wavecrest Laboratories on their 35 KW imbedded electric motor is over 700 lb-ft of torque.

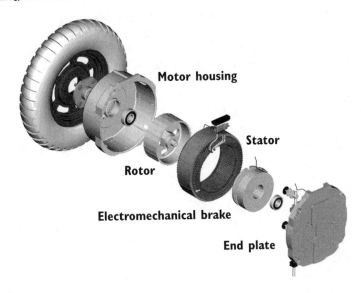

Motor housing

Stator

Rotor

Electromechanical brake

End plate

FIGURE I.4 THE WHEEL IS THE MOTOR. The embedded electric motor operates in four modes: forward, reverse, as a motor, as a generator. No need for transmission, axle or drive train while delivering more torque than a large pick up truck. Photo courtesy UQM Technologies, Inc.

The vehicle is now not only capable of true four-wheel drive, but it has four "motors," one at each wheel. If one motor fails there are three more to carry the load. In addition, all wheels are now unencumbered and can be steered fully because there is no need for an axle, greatly improving maneuverability. Developers of the imbedded electric technology claim that there is marked improvement in traction, braking and acceleration. The added weight at each wheel is only 35 pounds.

The embedded electric motors go from functioning as a motor to functioning as a generator when the brakes are applied. This accomplishes two things. The energy of braking is now turned into electricity and sent back to recharge the battery bank, it is not wasted as heat. The other thing "regenerative braking" does is improve the braking response itself, making the vehicle safer.

These wheel embedded motors are rated in the 25 KW to 35 KW range. For example the GM version is 25 KW with a pair delivering about 180 HP, and according to spokesmen for GM, will provide an improvement in torque of 60% over a comparable gasoline engine powered vehicle. Wavecrest Laboratories of Dulles, Virginia have developed a version at

35 KW, which delivers 737 lb-ft of torque and has a microprocessor controller to analyze vehicle performance and deliver energy to precisely match the load requirements at the wheel. In bad weather or muddy conditions, the wheel with the traction gets the power.

The Small Diesel Engine

For cruising and for charging the battery bank, the hybrid uses a small (1.25 liter - 2 liter) diesel engine. Let's say "advanced" diesel because in the U.S., the diesel still has a reputation of being noisy and spewing smoke.

Advances in diesel technology have resulted in clean and quiet engines while retaining the considerable advantages of diesel technology. This is evidenced by the fact that in Europe, diesel engines are used in 85% of the luxury car market and 50% of the auto market overall compared with less than 1% of the U.S. market.

The considerable advantages of diesel are: fuel flexibility, better fuel efficiency, more power, more durability and potentially more environmentally friendly.

Fuel flexibility: The diesel is a compression ignition technology, as opposed to spark ignition; the fuel is exploded under the high pressure of the cylinder. As such, it can use a variety of fuels including non-fossil TCP fuel oil or even unrefined restaurant grease.

Better fuel efficiency: Diesel fuel itself contains about 11% more energy than an equal amount of gasoline; in addition, the diesel engine burns the fuel more efficiently resulting in the same power output on 30% to 60% less fuel. Numerous diesel models now get over 60 mpg: Audi A2 at 87 mpg, VW Caddy 1.9 TDI at 60 mpg, VW Polo 1.4 TDI at 78 mpg and the Opel-ECO 5 Speedster at 92.6 mpg.

An illustration of the difference between diesel and gasoline is the VW Jetta, which is produced with both a gasoline and a diesel engine. With the gasoline engine, it gets 26 mpg; the diesel engine gets 38 mpg, an increase in mileage of 75%. In addition, the diesel model has more torque, reduced maintenance and longer engine life.

More power: At lower engine speeds the diesel has more power than a gasoline engine of the same displacement.

More Durable: Diesel engines are built more ruggedly. They have a longer period of time between recommended service and periodic maintenance checks, and the diesel is designed to go at least 200,000 miles, with many going 400,000 and more.

More Environmentally Friendly: This book calls for the elimination of *fossil* diesel fuels, instead utilizing other forms of liquid fuel which are not only produced from renewable sources, but do not contain sulfur. In any event, the days of noxious fumes and belching smoke are over because of advances in the technology. Diesel engines emit less carbon dioxide and fewer hydrocarbons than gasoline engines, and because of the greater mileage per gallon, less fuel is used. On top of this, diesels can burn "non-fossil diesel" in lieu of crude-oil derived diesel fuel. Non-fossil diesel is carbon neutral (see chart page 82) and puts out far less pollution than even the cleanest of gasoline engines, with the exception of NO_x.

The Enabling Diesel Technologies

High pressure turbocharged direct injection: Turbocharged direct injection (TDI) increases the combustion efficiency dramatically, resulting in greater fuel efficiency. This is also referred to as "advanced lean burn" technology. TDI typically increases mileage by 25%-40%.

Regenerative particulate filters: Pioneered by Peugeot, these filters are able to clean the exhaust fumes of more than 95% of the particulate matter. They also are able to regenerate themselves as you drive by recirculating and burning the trapped carbon.

Nitrogen reformers: By injecting hydrogen into the exhaust stream and reforming the gases, nitrogen oxide emissions are greatly reduced. NO_x emissions are smog producing gases and one of the areas where more progress needs to be made for diesel technology to be truly clean.

Variable valve actuation: Developed by Fiat, this improvement results in greater efficiency and less internal noise, which was a problem with the old diesels.

Hydraulic Drive train

A line carrying hydraulic fluid transfers power from the engine to the wheels without a transmission, axle, differential or drive train. In addition, power can be stored during braking by using the same hydraulic fluid to compress a gas, such as nitrogen, in an accumulator. Without a great deal of additional expense, this new innovation is capable of increasing mileage by over 50%[4]

New Battery Technology

Past attempts at electric vehicles were not successful, at least partially because of the penalty in weight and space for the lead-acid battery bank. A PDHEV will need 15 kWh of electrical storage capacity to go 60 miles. Using lead-acid, the battery would weigh over 900 pounds and have a volume of approximately 16 cubic feet. Advances in battery technology promise to decrease the weight from 900 down to less than 100 pounds and do it in much less volume.

With the capacity to go 60 miles, do all stop and go driving and accelerate on the highway using electricity, the diesel engine only needs to be started when cruising at highway speeds.

Lithium Chemistries

The cathode material of lithium-ion batteries now on the market requires expensive electronic circuitry in order to keep the batteries from overheating when being recharged. The overheating problem limits the size that the batteries can be made and is still a safety concern. Researchers at MIT have now reported that they may have solved that problem with new cathode materials that conduct extremely well without overheating. They expect the material to be available in early 2005.[5]

Water Chemistries

In a departure from the expense and overheating problems of lithium, researchers have developed a rechargeable version of the popular alkaline-type batteries. Referred to as zinc matrix, these batteries are a safe,

---

[4]At a Society of Automotive Engineers World Congress held in Detroit in February 2004, the EPA showed the first hydraulic hybrid SUV. The increased cost for this modification is $600, the increase in mileage was 55%.

[5]Gorman, J. "Bigger, Cheaper, Safer Batteries: New Material Charges Up Lithium-ion Battery Work." *Science News*, 21 Sept 2002: 196-197.

polymer-based, water-chemistry, rechargeable alkaline technology. Developers claim a capacity six times that of lead-acid batteries and four times that of nickel metal hydrides.[6]

Battery Technology			
Battery Type	Specific Energy Wh/kg (gravimetric)	Energy Density Wh/liter (volumetric)	Weight for 15 kWh storage
Fuel Cells for comparison	60 average now 120 best now 200 future	215	—
Lead-acid	35	80	940 pounds
Alkaline	50	145	660 pounds
NiCad	55	150	600 pounds
NiMetal Hydride	67	240	500 pounds
Lithium-ion	107-160	250	206 pounds
Lithium-polymer	125-150	—	220 pounds
Lithium-sulfur	350 600 projected	—	94 pounds 55 lbs projected
Zinc Matrix Polymer Based Rechargeable Alkaline	180-240		140-180 pounds

FIGURE 1.5
Compared to lead-acid, newer technology batteries deliver more power for the weight.

[6]*Zinc Matrix Technology at a Glance*, Zinc Matrix Power, Inc. June 2004 <www.zmp.com>

THE CASE FOR THE PDHEV

No new infrastructure required: The PDHEV is designed around existing vehicles now being manufactured - the SUV, passenger car and light truck - so no new industry retooling is required. The PDHEVs are nothing more than existing vehicles that are modified and improved to give much better performance. The small diesel engine could burn clean, locally produced non-fossil oil, and the battery bank could be recharged from on-site, high-temperature fuel cells or grid electricity.

Improved performance: The PDHEV is powered on the highway with a small diesel engine, but as additional power is needed to pass, the electric motors kick in with 180-200 horse power to give immediate acceleration. Once you have passed, the electric motors turn off automatically and you revert to the small diesel at cruising speed and recharging the batteries for the next time additional power is needed.

When driving in deep snow, off road or other very low speed, high torque, high traction situations, the PDHEV features an electric motor at each wheel that is electronically controlled to give the precise amount of power to each wheel according to how much traction is needed. The amount of torque is greater than what is now available on the larger muscle, dual-wheel pickups. If a motor should malfunction, there are three more as back up.

Marketable to the U.S. consumer: According to manufacturers, the diesel hybrids coming onto the U.S. market in 2004 will be successfully marketed because they are full-sized SUVs and trucks. Advertising departments are structuring their appeal to the SUV and truck owner, not the environmentally conscious consumer. The hybrid delivers to both consumer groups; the PDHEV does the same, but with even more advantages.

Cost considerations: Figure 1.6 dramatically illustrates the savings in the difference in gasoline mileage between a traditional vehicle and a PDHEV. The average family traveling 20,000 miles per year will purchase 67 gallons of liquid fuel for a PDHEV compared to 1,000 gallons currently. The additional initial cost to purchase a PDHEV has a payback due to lower fuel and maintenance costs and would single-handedly eliminate the trade deficit for foreign oil. Also, the additional cost is commensurate with the increased value of the vehicle. The diesel engine will go for 300,000 or more miles, and the embedded electric motors give improved performance.

FIGURE 1.6 If all passenger vehicles in the U.S. were PDHEVs, we could travel for a year on 10 billion gallons of fuel compared to 140 billion gallons currently. The chart illustrates comparative mileage.

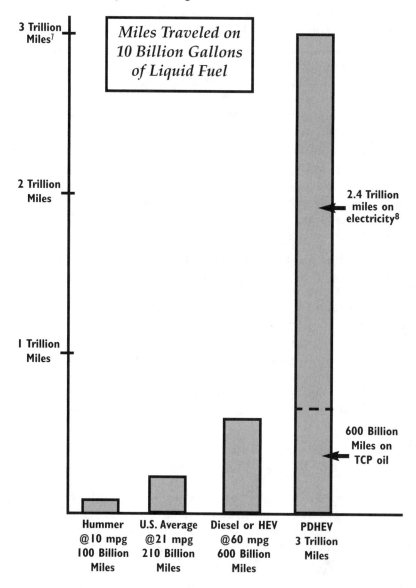

Miles Traveled on 10 Billion Gallons of Liquid Fuel

3 Trillion Miles[7]

2 Trillion Miles

1 Trillion Miles

2.4 Trillion miles on electricity[8]

600 Billion Miles on TCP oil

| Hummer @10 mpg 100 Billion Miles | U.S. Average @21 mpg 210 Billion Miles | Diesel or HEV @60 mpg 600 Billion Miles | PDHEV 3 Trillion Miles |

[7]Three trillion miles is the approximate total passenger vehicle miles for the U.S. for one year.

[8]The PDHEV would use 600 Billion kWh of grid or stationary fuel cell electricity.
80% of all miles driven (2.4 Trillion miles) are trips of less than 60 miles, the range for the PDHEV on battery power. 20% of the mileage (600 billion miles) would use the small diesel at cruising speeds.

The hydrogen fuel cell vehicle would be designed around the same platform, using embedded electric motors and battery packs with regenerative braking, as the PDHEV. If the hydrogen economy does become a reality someday, the small diesel will simply be replaced with a fuel cell; everything else will remain the same.

Energy Losses Comparing Hydrogen Fuel Cell Vehicle to Plug In Diesel Hybrid Electric Vehicle

The process starts with electricity from the grid or from a high-temperature fuel-cell (SOFC) on site. Figure 1.7 follows the energy on two paths: one path to operate the hydrogen fuel cell vehicle (HFCV) the other path to operate the PDHEV.

To operate the HFCV the electricity is first used to power an electrolyzer which passes the electrical current through water to produce hydrogen gas. Electrolyzers function at about 75% to 80% efficiency and are expensive machines to purchase and maintain (20% to 25% loss in electrolysis).

Hydrogen gas, at standard temperature and pressure, is then piped to a compressor where it is compressed in numerous stages up to 10,000 PSI. Compressors require additional electrical energy to operate and are expensive machines to acquire initially. (15% loss at the compressor).

It may be necessary to transfer the hydrogen in bulk to the consumer which is an energy intensive process because the hydrogen does not have high volumetric energy content. It may take 20-30 percent of the equivalent energy value of the hydrogen to transport it any great distance. We will figure somewhat less loss here. (2% to 20% loss for bulk transport)

Hydrogen must be stored on board the vehicle in addition to being stored in bulk. There is opportunity for leaking here but the main problem is getting enough hydrogen in terms of weight in a small enough volume. At 10,000 PSI, the hydrogen will still take up considerably more space than an equal amount of energy in the form of diesel fuel, for example. Storage tanks capable of keeping hydrogen at that kind of pressure are expensive. (1% loss from leakage in filling)

The hydrogen fuel is next piped to the fuel cell where it is used to make electricity at 40% to 50% efficiency. Fuel cells are very expensive at present and their durability is unknown. The lost energy is in the form of heat with water as a by-product. The fuel cell generates

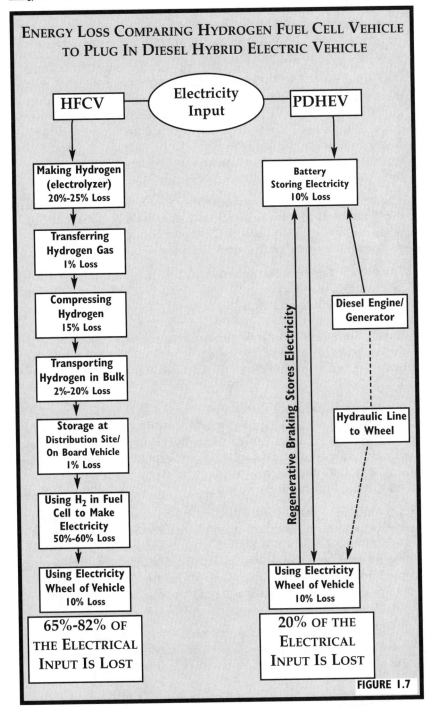

ENERGY LOSS COMPARING HYDROGEN FUEL CELL VEHICLE TO PLUG IN DIESEL HYBRID ELECTRIC VEHICLE

HFCV

Electricity Input

PDHEV

Making Hydrogen (electrolyzer) 20%-25% Loss

Transferring Hydrogen Gas 1% Loss

Compressing Hydrogen 15% Loss

Transporting Hydrogen in Bulk 2%-20% Loss

Storage at Distribution Site/ On Board Vehicle 1% Loss

Using H₂ in Fuel Cell to Make Electricity 50%-60% Loss

Using Electricity Wheel of Vehicle 10% Loss

Battery Storing Electricity 10% Loss

Regenerative Braking Stores Electricity

Diesel Engine/ Generator

Hydraulic Line to Wheel

Using Electricity Wheel of Vehicle 10% Loss

65%-82% OF THE ELECTRICAL INPUT IS LOST

20% OF THE ELECTRICAL INPUT IS LOST

FIGURE 1.7

electricity, which is where we started out. The electricity drives an embedded electric motor that operates at 90% efficiency.

In the case of the PDHEV, the electricity is used initially to charge the battery pack. AC to DC conversion will lose a small amount of electricity, but there are no other conversions between the battery and the embedded electric motors. Importantly, when the vehicle brakes, the energy is not lost as heat; it is used to charge the battery. Much more energy is regained here, than lost in conversion. The assumption is that the original electricity is generated with wind or high temperature fuel cells, not coal or nuclear.

The battery pack can be charged several other ways. The small diesel engine is coupled to a generator, which charges the batteries when under way. The other possibility is to install solar cells on the vehicle which would charge the batteries whenever the sun shines.

The diesel engine is also used to power the wheels directly with a hydraulic drive, which is equipped with an accumulator that also stores energy from braking.

Conclusion: Between the origination and traction, 65% to 82% of the energy is lost when using the HFC vehicle. The same amount of energy, when used in the PDHEV, is lost at the far lower rate of 15% to 20%.

In addition, some of the technologies employed in the HFC vehicle scenario require considerable research and development to overcome technical hurdles. In contrast, the small diesel engine is a proven and mature technology. Battery technologies have come a long way since the reliance on lead-acid types of a few years ago but still need further improvements.

A complicating factor for the hydrogen scenario is that it is being used as a cover for political agendas that are really interested in perpetuating a reliance on oil and nuclear because of the opportunity for enormous short-term profits. This factor needs to be separated from those who are operating in good faith promoting hydrogen as a clean energy carrier as a possible solution to energy problems.

The use of hydrogen for transportation does not appear to be a very good thermodynamic pathway from primary energy to traction on a roadway. There are much better ways to do it.

FUEL CELLS

Fuel cells are electrochemical devices that use hydrogen gas or a hydrogen rich liquid fuel which is reacted with an oxidant, usually oxygen from the air, to produce electricity, heat and water. This is an electrochemical process, not a combustion process, so there is no flue and very few emissions. If pure hydrogen is used for the fuel, and if the hydrogen comes from renewable sources (not fossil fuels or nuclear), there are no emissions.

The diagram (Figure 1.8) shows a generalized representation of the fuel cell process. Hydrogen enters the fuel cell and encounters a catalyst, such as platinum, at the anode which breaks the hydrogen atom into an electron and a proton. The electron is routed into an external circuit where it does work as an electrical current. The proton migrates through a polymer membrane within the fuel cell and is joined up at the cathode with oxygen from outside air and the electrons, which have completed their circuit, to form water.

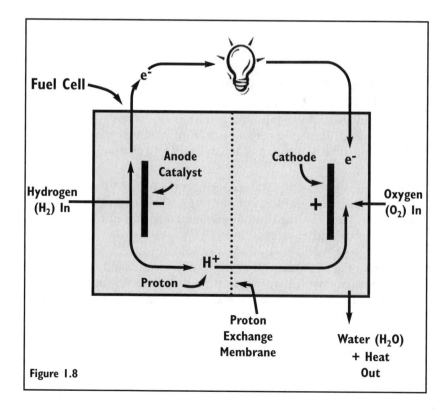

Figure 1.8

This reaction is highly exothermic (gives off heat), especially in the high temperature fuel cells. The heat can be recovered for uses such as space heating, domestic hot water or even industrial process heat. In high temperature fuel cells, heat can be recovered at over 1000°F which can be further put to use by driving a steam turbine to produce more electricity. This is called "combined cycle" electrical production and can raise the fuel to electric efficiency of the fuel cell to over 80%.

The fuel cell converts fuel much more efficiently than a power plant with fuel to electric efficiencies over 50% and fuel to recoverable heat at about 40%. This gives an overall efficiency for the fuel cell of about 90%, compared to 35% for central coal fired plants (see Figure 1.12).

Other advantages to fuel cell power is that the fuel cell operates on site, quietly, with no emissions to the atmosphere, providing power that is more reliable and of better quality.

Types of Fuel Cells

Fuel cells may be divided into three categories according to intended use: vehicle power plants, portable power and stationary power. We will add a fourth, microbial, for the sake of interest.

Vehicle Power Plants and Small Stationary Use
Proton Exchange Membrane (PEM) Fuel Cell

This technology requires pure hydrogen gas as the fuel. If other fuels are to be used, they must first be reformed, which means that the hydrogen must be removed and separated before entering the fuel cell.

PEM fuel cells operate at low temperature (180°-200°F) with or without heat recovery in the form of hot water. This temperature is high enough for space heating or domestic hot water but not high enough for steam or industrial process heat.

The time for the PEM fuel cell to respond to the demand for electricity is very short, almost instantaneous, so it is well suited for use in vehicles although it is also a likely candidate for small stationary power applications.

Portable Electronics and Vehicle Power
Direct Methanol Fuel Cell (DMFC)
The architecture of the Direct Methanol Fuel Cell is similar to the PEM except that the hydrogen is generated directly within the cell from methanol (methyl alcohol). There is no need for an outside reformer. Methanol is a hydrogen rich fuel, at 12% hydrogen by weight, as well as being easy to store and inexpensive to purchase.

There are 35 companies, primarily consumer electronics manufacturers, with DMFC development programs. The first fuel cell powered laptops and cell phones will be on the market in late 2004.

Laptop Computers

Cameras and Cell Phones

Camcorders

Personal Electronics

Scooters

FIGURE 1.9 A few of the many fuel cell powered products developed for commercialization. Personal electronics and camera and cell phone photos courtesy Medis Technologies. Fuji fuel cell powered notebook computer photo courtesy Fuji. Yamaha Motors FC06 scooter courtesy Yamaha Motors.

With further development, DMFCs are thought to also have application for vehicles as an option to fuel cells that require pure hydrogen as a fuel. Methanol is 12% hydrogen by weight, which makes it a fairly good hydrogen carrier, perhaps even better than compressing hydrogen gas. Methanol is currently used in industry to a great extent and has a wholesale cost of less than 50 cents a gallon. As with TCP oil, methanol can be manufactured from waste and biomass.

High Temperature Stationary
Solid Oxide Fuel Cell (SOFC)

SOFCs are a type of high temperature fuel cell that will accept just about any form of hydrocarbon as a fuel source; in this case it could be fed the #2 fuel oil from the TC process or methanol. The fuel cell converts the fuel oil into electricity at over 50% efficiency and produces high temperature process heat at over 1000°F, of which about 40% can be recovered for industrial uses or for space heating. This makes the SOFC over 90% efficient with few emissions because the fuel is electrochemically converted; there is no combustion in the process. Since the power is generated on site, as opposed to a central site 300 miles away, the heat can be recovered where it is needed.

FIGURE 1.10   250 KW high temperature fuel cell. Photo courtesy of Fuel Cell Energy, Inc. Large enough to serve a village or large apartment complex.

SOFCs can be made in a wide range of sizes from 1 KW on up to 2 MW of electrical output. A 1 KW unit would produce about 8700 kWh per year, which is enough for a small home or apartment. The average household consumption in the U.S. is about 10,000 kWh per year. Units could be sized to serve a home, a neighborhood, a small town or an industrial complex using buried cable for distribution.

Distributed generation (DG), which simply means generating the power on site, has several advantages. Heat can be recovered and used as space heat, for domestic hot water or to run turbines to generate more electricity. Other benefits of DG using fuel cells are that the cleanly generated power is more reliable and of better quality. The systems are modular in nature, meaning that with many smaller but identical units as opposed to one large central coal fired or nuclear plant, they are easier and faster to install and easier to fund. DG also means that the electrical distribution grid, with all of its reliability problems, expense and insecurity, is no longer necessary.

COMPARING FUEL CELLS

	Stationary SOFC MCFC	Vehicle, Portable PEM DMFC	Alkaline Fuel Cells
Start Up Load Response	Slow (15-30 Min.) Slow to Respond	Fast Quick to Respond	Fast Quick to Respond
Operating Temperature	1000-1700° F	180-200° F	150-180° F
Fuel to Electric Efficiency	45-52%	30%	50%
Heat Recovery Overall Efficiency	40% 85-92%	30% 60%	
Catalyst	Non-precious metal	Platinum	Non-precious metal
Current Cost per kW to install	$2500-$1200	$2000+	$300
Projected Cost	$1000 MCFC $400 SOFC	$50	$50
Longevity	40,000 hours	200-5000 hours	5,000 hours
Fuel Requirement	Any hydrocarbon, alcohol, DME	Pure hydrogen	Pure hydrogen
Capacity Range	1 KW to megawatt	micro to 50 KW	3 KW to 50KW

FIGURE 1.11

Microbial Fuel Cells

Microbial fuel cells enable the direct conversion of carbohydrates (sugars) to electricity. With the identification of organisms, such as *Rhodoferax ferrireducens*, bacteria that use iron in respiration, researchers have been able to make a fuel cell that uses ocean bottom muck as a primary fuel.

The bacteria consume sugars in the environment for energy and free up electrons in the process. Normally the bacteria would pass the electron along to iron compounds in the environment, but researchers have been able to substitute a graphite electrode and, in effect, get the bacteria to make a continuous supply (but in very small amounts) of electricity.

Previous attempts to do this were only able to capture about 1% of the electrons; this new discovery could increase the percentage to around 80%. The importance of this process is that carbohydrates and sugars are everywhere in the environment including waste streams.

Figure 1.12

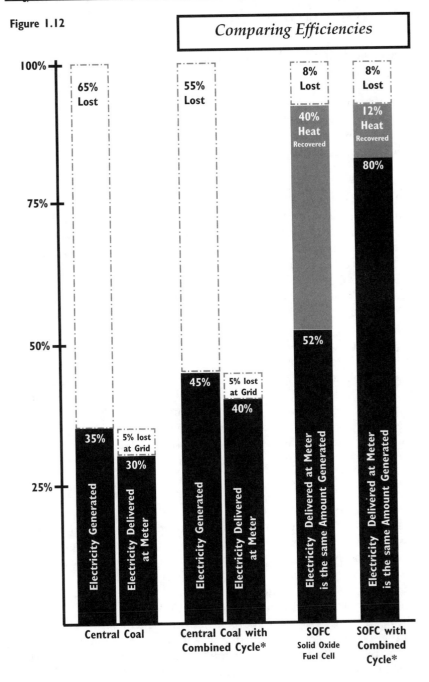

Comparing Efficiencies

*Combined cycle uses recovered heat to generate additional electricity.

Sun To Heat and Sun to Electricity Technologies

The ancient Greeks, 2000 years ago, were able to use the sun's energy very effectively in designing their homes and public spaces. Likewise, the Anasazi culture designed and built their dwellings 700 years ago to take advantage of the sun to heat massive adobe walls that would re-radiate heat into the living space at night. Capturing heat from the sun is not a new concept, it has been around a long time. We incorporate it here because it is practical and cost effective.

Solar Thermal
Collectors Capture The Sun's Heat

The amount of heat intercepted by the footprint of an average home is over ten times the heating requirement of that home. On average, 570,000 BTUs of solar energy fall on each square foot of the U.S. each year. Solar thermal systems are simply an effort to collect some of that heat, store it and later transfer it to the interior space of the building for space heating or for domestic hot water.

Flat Plate Solar Collector

A flat plate collector is nothing more than a roof mounted black absorber plate with copper tubes welded to the back side, a frame with a glass covering to allow the heat to build up and insulation behind to prevent heat loss. A liquid is circulated through the collector absorbing the sun's heat and transferring it to where it can be used or stored. The amount of heat that can be collected and stored by using a solar collector is 25% to 50% of the total amount falling on the surface of the collector.

Ground Mounted Solar (GS)

A system representing a radical departure from the roof mounted flat plate collector is proposed by retired physicist, Dr. Mel Prueitt, from Los Alamos, New Mexico. This system, also referred to as Solawatt®, consists of a flexible plastic panel, which is on a roll about 4-5 feet wide and could be of any length. The panel has channels through which water flows in contact with the ground and two layers of optical grade plastic covering with separation air cavities. The inner panel is coated with a special selective coating that lets infrared radiation through and prevents the re-radiation of the collected heat at night. The panel is rolled out directly on the ground, which then becomes part of the heat storage feature of the system. The circulating water is pumped through

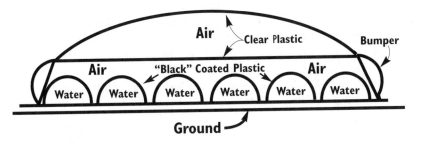

Figure 1.13 Section view of Ground Mounted Solar (GS) showing channels for water and insulating air spaces above. Total width is about five feet. Diagram compliments of Solar Energy Limited, Santa Fe, New Mexico.

a hot water reservoir where the heat is stored. The plastic material is Tefzel®, from DuPont Corporation, a UV resistant and optical grade plastic, having a useful life of thirty years. At the end of its life the plastic could be sold to the local thermal conversion (TCP) plant for conversion to fuel oil.

Prototype testing has shown that this collector can capture up to 75% of the solar radiant heat, which would be equivalent to the efficiency of the flat plate collector. The plastic panels would be mass produced in continuous rolls of any length for a fraction of the cost of the flat plate collector according to Prueitt. Instead of being limited to roof space, it could be installed by the acre or square mile for under $3 per square foot, compared to flat plate collectors at a cost of $15-$20 per square foot plus $5-$10 installation cost.

Passive Solar Potential
Designing Buildings To Capture Free Heat
As with solar thermal systems, passive solar is simply an attempt to capture some of the 570,000 BTUs per square foot per year that fall on the earth's surface. By giving some thought initially to the building design, or by retrofitting existing buildings, a substantial portion of that energy can be captured. This is accomplished by placing glass surfaces so sunlight enters the building, where it heats a sun space and can be stored in architectural features of the space, such as a dark stone floor or a wall containing thermal mass. By intelligent design, 50% of space heating requirements, even in cold climates, can be met using passive solar features.

The potential is difficult to define because it depends so much on how willing people are, or how much incentive people are given, to incorporate passive solar features into their homes and places of work. A solarium is an example of incorporating a simple design feature to cut heating requirements by as much as half. By placing 240 square feet of insulated glass on the south side, about 20 million free BTUs are captured in this 40' X 10' greenroom/solarium (photo below). In summer months, the overhang is designed to keep direct sunlight out of the room.

Another advantage of the solarium is that this airspace serves as an air envelope, preventing any air infiltration into the main living space of the home. Infiltration of cold outside air is the main source of heat loss in a home. The wintertime room temperature is allowed to swing from 50°F at night to 85°F on a sunny day in the solarium. When the sun comes out, even on days of extreme cold, the temperature immediately rises to 80°F in this space. Warm air rises in the solarium and is allowed into the main living space through two fan assisted transfer air vents high in the space. Return air is circulated back from the main living space through vents located along the floor of the sunroom.

This design feature also allows the main living areas to be more comfortable in the winter because the interior walls heat up. Regardless of the actual room air temperature, it is more comfortable to be in a space with warm surfaces surrounding you than cold surfaces.

Although not everyone can grow bananas like Amory Lovins,[9] flowers often bloom all winter...a welcome sight in far northern Wisconsin where the snow can be four feet deep and the temperatures can dip to minus 20°F.

Photovoltaics (PV)
The Direct Conversion of Sunlight to Electricity
Photovoltaics refers to the direct conversion of sunlight to electricity. When sunlight, the radiant energy from the sun called "photons," strikes the surface of certain special types of semi-conducting material, electrons are jolted loose from the material. The electrons are then able to move to an adjacent layer of material where they flow freely -- as an electrical current. There are three classes of photovoltaic (PV) material: crystalline silicon, amorphous silicon and dye sensitized solar cells.

PV is the ultimate in distributed generation of electricity because the sun shines everywhere, and a PV array can be installed just about anyplace that electricity is needed -- even in the remotest locations. PV has the advantage of being relatively simple to install and operate with no moving parts and requires very little upkeep or maintenance. Once installed, the cost to operate and maintain the system is low.

PV systems are also modular in that larger systems are nothing more than many of the same modules of smaller systems put together. This makes it easy to design the right sized system and to change the system based upon future needs without having to pay a cost penalty.

Crystalline Silicon PV
As the most mature of the three PV technologies, it is known that crystalline silicon solar cells continue to perform for over 20 years, without losing capacity and pretty much trouble free. The cells are made with very pure silicon that is grown as a crystal and sawed into thin wafers which are wired together to form the solar array.

---

[9]Amory Lovins is the Director of the Rocky Mountain Institute in Snowmass, Colorado whose 4000 SF well designed office space uses virtually no outside heat source.

Silicon is considered a semi-conductor, which means that it doesn't normally conduct electricity, but under certain conditions, it will. The crystal must be defect free, or the electrons will become trapped in the crystalline structure of the silicon. For this reason, they are relatively expensive to make. The cost for the solar cells themselves is about $40 per square foot, and they convert sunlight striking them at about 10-15% efficiency.

The balance of the system -- batteries, charge controllers, cables, inverter, switches -- add about 80% to the collector cost. The cost to provide PV power to a home in a remote village in the undeveloped world is calculated at $622. This is enough power to run lights, a radio and a spinning wheel, for example. On a much different scale, a recently completed project in Hayward, California uses over 100,000 square feet of collectors to power a significant portion of the electrical needs for the state college at a cost of $7 million for installation.

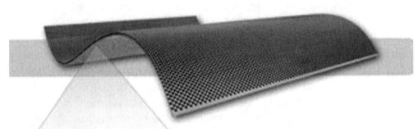

FIGURE 1.14 New generations of photovoltaic cells are flexible, lightweight and cost less than crystalline silicon types. Photo courtesy of Spheral Solar Technology.

Thin Film Amorphous Silicon

Amorphous silicon cells, also called "thin-film," are not crystalline and, therefore, less expensive to make. The amorphous semi-conductor material can be applied in very thin coatings to a substrate, such as plastic or stainless steel. Amorphous silicon cells are less efficient, but are also less expensive -- the cost to produce the same number of kWh is about the same as crystalline cells. Because thin film solar does not require a mounting frame, it can be applied directly to steel roofing.

Uni-Solar, a Michigan manufacturer, has developed a flexible, lightweight and easy to install thin film product in rolls of up to one and a half miles long that can be applied in lieu of steel roofing. It serves as roofing material or can be incorporated as other architectural features of a building and operates at about 8% efficiency. It can also be installed as a retrofit on steel roofs. Pictured below, the solar roof atop the Californians for Alternatives to Toxics building in Eureka utilized the Uni-Solar system roof.

Dye Sensitized Solar Cells (DSSC)

Researchers on three continents are now developing totally new kinds of semi-conductor materials based in polymers instead of the expensive and difficult to manufacture crystalline silicon. Scientists are predicting costs will come down to one tenth the current costs for PV cells while achieving comparable efficiencies.

Recent developments in nano-technology will have implications for solar cells. Organic dyes, which absorb light, are deposited on a nanoporous substrate of metal oxides, such as titanium dioxide, TiO_2. These new cells, called dye sensitized solar cells (DSSC), mimic photosynthesis, the process in nature where green plants are able to capture the sun's energy and use it for metabolic processes.

These cells will be manufactured on continuous polymer film and will not require a frame to mount; in fact, they will be adhered directly to roofs or building structures. Researchers believe that this type of cell can eventually reach efficiencies of an ideal conventional PV cell, 20-30%, at a fraction of the cost.[10]

---

[10]Gratzel, Michael. "Applied Physics: Solar Cells to Dye For." *Nature* 06 February 2003:586-7

New Innovations

Another innovation is the organic or polymer solar cells being developed at the University of Arizona, University of California (Berkeley), Switzerland, and at Pusan University in Korea, that can be sprayed onto roofs or even printed onto clothing. Considered impossible a few years ago, research in conducting plastics has changed that point of view, predicting solar cells of 10% efficiency at one tenth the current PV cell costs.[11]

Ground Mounted Solar/Refrigerant Turbine (GSRT)
Electricity for less than 2 cents per kWh.

GSRT is an adaptation of the ground mounted thermal system described previously (page 41). The panel has channels through which water flows in contact with the ground and two layers of optical grade plastic covering with separation air cavities. The panel is rolled out directly on the ground, which then becomes part of the heat storage feature of the system. The circulating water does two things: it conducts solar heat into the ground, and it serves to evaporate a refrigerant fluid in a heat exchanger. The expanding refrigerant then turns a small gas turbine, which is connected to a generator that produces electricity. The system will produce electricity 24 hours a day by pulling stored heat from the ground at night. One square mile of GSRT (640 acres) would generate enough electricity for about 60,000 homes or a community of 130,000 people. At wholesale rates (3 cents per kWh) the electricity is worth $20 million dollars, 100-150 times the value of whatever might be grown on the land. The plastic material is UV resistant and optical grade, having a useful life of thirty years.

Performance data for the GSRT system comes from the inventor and is based upon prototypes operated in New Mexico and computer simulations. The system is unproven for lack of funding, but promises to be able to generate electricity for under two cents per kWh.

---

[11]"Solar Cells Go Organic" Science Technology Quarterly. *The Economist.* 20 June 2002.

WIND GENERATORS

Wind, like sunlight, is free and abundant. Unlike solar, however, commercial development of wind has matured to a point where today, wind is the lowest cost method to produce electricity. One 2.3 MW wind generator, a size available from all major manufacturers, under normal operating conditions will produce $564,000 worth of electricity per year.[12] Contracts for bulk power from large wind farms are now being negotiated for under three cents per kWh, in some cases. Wind can compete with any and all other forms of power generation and does it cleanly. The goal is to lower the cost of wind generated power to below three cents in low wind speed areas.

The wind turbines themselves are getting more efficient and larger every year. Ten years ago, 500 KW was considered a large wind generator having a hub height of 150 feet and a blade diameter of 120 feet. Today, 3.6 MW units are common (hub height 260 feet, blade diameter 300 feet), 5 MW units are in development and 10 MW units are on the drawing boards.

A 2.3 MW unit has a rotor blade diameter of 270 feet; the nacelle, which contains the generator, gearing and controllers, is over 50 feet in length (about the size of a school bus) and weighs 300,000 pounds including the blades at 114,000 pounds. All of this is on top of a steel tubular tower 200-260 feet from ground to hub. The offshore model spins at 17 revolutions per minute, the onshore model at 11 revolutions per minute, a much lower speed than the wind generators of even a few years ago, making the units much quieter and less of a problem for migrating birds. A modern wind generator has a system of sophisticated monitors that sense, and in some cases control, about 300 variables.

---

[12]At average retail rates of $.08 per kWh.

Research and development is now focused on refinements -- ways to further reduce costs and ways to improve efficiency of the turbines at low wind speeds.

Blade design is a critical factor in wind economics as they are 25% of the total cost, can weigh well over 100,000 pounds and affect energy output a great deal.

One approach that promises to cut blade costs drastically is to design the wind generator so the blades are downwind of the tower. Two factors come into play: the blades can be allowed to flex more being down wind but air turbulence around the tower must mitigated. Enhanced computer modeling has enabled designers to overcome the turbulence problem and with more flex allowed, the blades can be made much less expensively and with less critical stress parameters.

Research coordinated by the National Renewable Energy Laboratory (NREL) in

Do Wind Generators Kill Birds?

Since the first devices with fast moving blades were installed on lattice towers in California 30 years ago, much progress has been made in reducing bird fatalities.

The blades of modern units only turn at 11-17 revolutions per minute, far slower than the old machines. Lattice towers, which were attractive perching spots for birds, have been replaced with solid tubular towers, greatly reducing bird kills.

The larger machines also mean that far fewer are used at a given site. They are also spaced much further apart than older wind farms.

According to the Union of Concerned Scientists, a recent study concluded that a vast majority of the birds killed in 2001 at U.S. wind farms were at older sites. Further, the number of bird fatalities at wind farms is a tiny fraction of the the estimated 200 million to 500 million annual bird fatalities attributed to human activity, such as vehicles, windows, power lines and house cats.

Golden, Colorado promises to make wind generators more efficient and less costly. NREL and various manufacturers are working together to develop new blade manufacturing processes, new materials, new blade shapes and more sophisticated testing protocols. Studies now underway at NREL explore new construction materials and ways to construct the tower on site as towers are becoming so large they are difficult to transport. In addition, new drive trains are being developed to increase turbine efficiency at low wind speeds as well as decrease cost and weight.

The Northern Power Systems configuration (Figure 1.15) improves reliability and lowers the cost of energy by eliminating the gearbox by using a direct drive.

The Global Energy Concepts drive train (Figure 1.16) is designed to operate efficiently at low wind speeds allowing wind generation to be economically feasible in more places.

FIGURE 1.15

FIGURE 1.16

The Clipper Windpower drive train (Figure 1.17) is 30% lighter than comparable sized units.

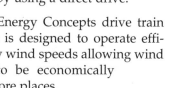

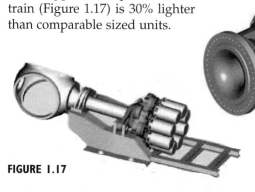

Photos: **U.S. Department of Energy. Wind Power Today & Tomorrow. March 2004.**

FIGURE 1.17

Wind energy is the fastest growing power technology in the world. In 2002, European countries installed $7 billion worth of wind generating equipment compared to less than half a billion dollars worth in the U.S. A contributing factor to the slow U.S. market is the uncertain status of the federal production tax credit that was established in 1992, which must be renewed every two years by an act of Congress. Currently, the U.S. has about 15% of the installed wind capacity; Europe has about 75%.

Denmark, a country about the size of Maine with a population of five million, exported $3 billion dollars worth of wind generators last year and holds 75% of the world market share. Denmark is home to four major wind generator manufacturers: Vestas, Neg-Micon (recently merged), Nordex and Bonus.[13]

---

[13]Danish Wind Industry Association. July 2004. ,www.windpower.org>

The Flying Wind Generator

A novel application of wind generation is the "flying wind generator," which would look something like the shell of a helicopter that would have generators instead of engines and would auto rotate in the wind at the end of a tether 15,000 to 30,000 feet in the air. The tether would also be a conductor through which the electricity would travel.

Proponents of the flying wind generator claim that the technical problem of a tether that long has been solved and cite the fifty or so drug surveillance balloons tethered at 15,000 feet altitude near the southern border of the U.S. as evidence. It is estimated that the lifecycle cost for such a machine would enable the production of electricity for about a cent or even less than one cent per kilowatt hour (kWh). This form of generation would not lend itself well to distributed generation because of FAA/airspace control requirements but could be placed in clusters in restricted airspace near metropolitan areas.

Optimum Wind Energy Conditions

There are two parameters regarding wind energy that are important: consistency (the wind blowing steadily) and speed (the wind blowing at a high rate of speed). As elevation increases, both of these factors are optimized. At 15,000 feet the conditions are very good, at 30,000 the conditions are about as good as it can get -- 100 mile an hour wind speeds with an 80% or 90% capacity factor. The extractable energy is a cubed function of the speed; twice the speed means eight times the energy. Five times the wind speed means 125 times the available energy. Raising the capacity factor from the expected 35% on the surface to 80-90% at 30,000 feet altitude increases the energy production by another 220%. One hundred twenty five times 2.2 gives a theoretical increase in electrical production of 275 times. For every kWh that a wind generator with given rotor diameter can produce on the ground, it should be able to produce 275 kWh (derated for air density) at 30,000 feet. A more realistic number would be in the range of 20 to 30 times as much as a ground-based generator, but still a lot more energy.

OCEAN SYSTEMS

Electricity from the movement of water

There are two basic types of ocean systems; one type captures energy from the up and down (vertical) motion of the waves, and the other captures energy in the moving mass (horizontal) of water, either tidal flow or ocean currents.

Wave systems

Wave energy conversion systems are typically moored just offshore and depend on a consistent wave front approaching the shore. The potential is large, when one considers the four thousand some miles of coast of the U.S., but the practical amount of electricity within reasonable distance of consumers is a different matter. Currently, seven companies world wide are bringing wave energy conversion systems to the market place.

Wavedragon is a tubular device that floats on the water surface and articulates as the waves move beneath it. Now being tested in Denmark, the developers claim their 4 MW unit will produce 35 million kWh per year at seven cents per kWh.

The Pelamis project (Figure 1.18) is a 30 MW wave farm covering one square kilometer and producing enough electricity to serve 20,000 homes. This would equate to 77 MW potential per square mile of ocean surface having sufficient energy in the wave fronts. In reality, wave farms would be disbursed, but for scale, a 100 mile x 100 mile area would accommodate a Pelamis system that could produce all of the electrical demand for the U.S.

FIGURE 1.18 Pelamis system consists of four segments, with a total length of 500 feet and a diameter of 12 feet. Each unit will produce 2.7 million kWh per year. Photo courtesy of Ocean Power Delivery Limited.

Ocean Tidal and Current Systems

These energy conversion systems either sit on the ocean floor where there is a tidal stream or a current flowing most of the time, or are suspended in the current. They can look something like a propeller wind generator, a vertical axis wind generator, a turbine, or they can use a hydroplane surface much like the wing of an airplane which is driven up and down by the flow of water past it. In any case, the fact that seawater is over 800 times as dense as air means that there is a great deal of kinetic energy available in an ocean or river current. An eight mile per hour ocean current would have about the same energy available as a 170 mile an hour wind speed. In a given area, an ocean current system can extract about 180 times as much energy as a wind system.

The "Stingray," built in Britain by Engineering Business, an offshore equipment designer and builder, uses 15 meter airfoil shaped hydroplanes that move up and down when the tidal stream flows past. The hydroplane arms then are forced to move up and down which in turn drives a hydraulic motor that generates electricity. The structure weighs 35 tons and rises 20 meters above the ocean floor. The Stingray flips over four times a day to catch the tidal currents both incoming and outgoing. There are 40 key locations around coastal Britain with enough energy in tidal streams to generate 25% of that nation's electricity.

Marine Current Turbines of London has developed another version of the tidal current energy extractor in the form of circular motion propeller type turbines with an installed capacity of 300 KW with projects located at Lynmouth, U.K. and off the coast of north Devon, U.K. Industry spokesmen predict a multi billion dollar industry in the near future.

In a project funded by New York City and the State of New York, 300 underwater turbines are to be installed in the East River between Roosevelt Island and Bronx, N.Y. (Figure 1.19) Verdant Power, a Virginia energy development company, is in the third and last stage of preparation for

FIGURE 1.19 Typical 37 KW turbine. The New York City project will install 300 such turbines.

installation of the "tidal turbines." With a tidal current of six mph, the units will provide 10 MW of electricity, enough for 8000 homes. The turbines have a blade diameter of 15 feet and will remain eight feet below the river surface so as not to interfere with boating. Mr. Trey Taylor, owner of Verdant Power, states that these turbines will be installed for about $2,000/KW and will produce power for seven cents per kWh. He expects the costs to drop to $1500 per installed KW in the future and to be able to produce energy for about five cents per kWh.

The San Francisco Board of Supervisors voted unanimously to fund a $2 million pilot project to examine harnessing the tidal stream under the Golden Gate Bridge where each tidal cycle pushes 400 billion gallons of water through the channel, enough recoverable energy to meet the city's electrical demand two times over. The system would not interfere with the busy shipping traffic in the area.[14]

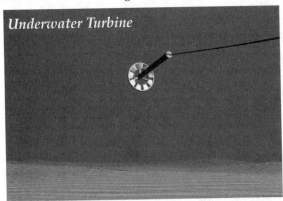

Underwater Turbine

FIGURE 1.20   Anchored in the Gulf Stream, 200 feet below the ocean surface off the east coast of the U.S., an underwater turbine harnesses energy from ocean currents. Photo courtesy of Florida Hydro Power & Light.

Underwater Turbines
Underwater turbines are similar to wind generators but are installed below the surface of the ocean and used to capture the energy of ocean currents, such as the Gulf Stream. Projects in various states of development are underway in the Philippines, Canada, the U.K., San Francisco Bay and off the Florida coast in the Gulf Stream.

14"San Francisco Weighs Harnessing Tides for Electricity" Reuters News Service. 8 May 2003. <http://www.planetark.org/dailynewsstory.cfm/newsid/20717/story.htm>

MORE WAYS TO PRODUCE CLEAN LIQUID FUELS

Since the great American love affair with the automobile began, we have relied on fossil oil to keep us on the go, but there are alternatives. An ideal liquid fuel would have the following characteristics.

- Easy and convenient to handle by the consumer
- Non toxic
- Easy to transport and store in bulk
- Easy to store on board a vehicle
- High energy content by volume
- Inexpensive
- Acquired and produced locally; a bonus feature would be that the process tended to solve societal problems instead of create them
- Safe, fumes lighter than air but not too volatile
- Clean, no sulfur, mercury or other pollutants. Should be carbon neutral
- No hidden costs; external costs should be paid for   by those who profit from the process and not shifted to the public or other people.

Gasoline and diesel fuel come close to being ideal energy carriers except for three of the items above: they are not inexpensive at $300+ per barrel,[15] they are not clean, and they come with many externalities, or hidden costs, associated with their acquisition and use. Dimitri Mendeleev (1834-1907), the Russian chemist who was first to propose a periodic chart of the elements, made a statement to the effect that burning oil was a foolish thing to do, that "it was akin to firing up the kitchen stove with bank notes." Mendeleev realized that petroleum could be a valuable material to use as a precursor for other end products, such as plastics and chemicals. Indeed, burning fossil petroleum is not necessary at all, much less a "wise" thing to be encouraging with government policy. Despite Mendeleev's advice, over 90% of the oil in the U.S. economy is burned with less than 10% converted into plastics and chemicals.

Cost effectiveness for any liquid fuel manufacturing process is a function of the price of oil, which is artificially set by OPEC (Organization

---

[15]The cost of Middle East oil breaks down roughly as follows: $6 to pump it, pipe it to port and transport it to the U.S., $3-$4 to refine it and distribute the gasoline, $40 to purchase it from an OPEC government, and about $250 in military expenditures to acquire it from Middle East sources.

of Petroleum Exporting Countries). OPEC does not want a price higher than $28 per barrel because they know that once it remains at that point for long, it becomes profitable to manufacture liquid fuels. They intentionally try to keep the price below $28 per barrel so countries remain dependent on them.

SOME PROBLEMS WITH HYDROGEN AS A FUEL

Hydrogen is not an ideal fuel.

Hydrogen is a very light gas, and in order to get enough of it in a confined space, it must be compressed to 5000 PSI or even 10,000 PSI. This extreme pressure is problematic for the average consumer in refueling because of safety concerns and the requirement for specialized fittings.

It is difficult and expensive to transport hydrogen in bulk for the same reasons that it is inconvenient for the average consumer to handle it. Hydrogen does not contain enough energy by VOLUME to transport it economically by truck. Special pipelines could be used, but they have their own set of difficulties and expense.

Hydrogen has a high-energy content by weight, but not by VOLUME. It is so light that even though it has a lot of energy by weight, it is difficult to confine very much of it in a reasonable volume. At 10,000 PSI, hydrogen still requires several times the volume of gasoline for the same amount of energy; plus, it takes energy to compress it.

Hydrogen is only clean if it is produced with renewable resources. If it is made with nuclear energy or fossil fuels, there is no point in making it at all. For many reasons, hydrogen is a good idea, but some politicians use hydrogen as a cover to continue the involvement of the fossil fuel and nuclear industries in the energy mix. With all of its technical problems, hydrogen is still a much better idea than continued reliance on oil or the continued taxpayer bailout of the nuclear industry, but we should be aware of the technical hurdles yet to be overcome.

There are numerous ways to derive energy-dense liquid fuels that are carbon neutral, clean burning and less expensive than fossil petroleum. We will look briefly at methanol synthesis, synthetic liquid fuels, fast pyrolysis and gas to liquid processes.

Methanol Synthesis

Methanol (methyl alcohol, CH_3-OH) meets most of the criteria for a good liquid fuel. Its energy content is less than gasoline or diesel,[16] but that is not necessarily a show stopper, especially when it is used in highly efficient vehicles or with fuel cells.

Methanol has some significant advantages as a liquid fuel: it can be made from waste and biomass, which are locally procured, and it can be produced relatively inexpensively. Although most methanol is now manufactured using natural gas as a feedstock, it can also be made using non-fossil fuel resources for comparable costs. Methanol wholesales at about 46 cents per gallon and retails for around a dollar.

Methanol is safer than gasoline (although both are poisonous to swallow) because it degrades in water more readily, and it does not contain carcinogens and mutagens as does gasoline. Gasoline contains highly mutagenic chemicals, such as benzene and toluene, which are also highly soluble in water. Compared to JP-8, a specially formulated type of diesel, methanol is benign. (See page 120 for a more detailed discussion of the hazards of JP-8.)

Transporting and distributing methanol is already being done to a large degree with six million tons per year sold in the U.S. alone. It is transported by rail cars, barges and by truck.

A new Swedish patented process for producing methanol uses waste streams from the pulp and paper manufacturing process. The process, called "black liquor gasification," is 66% efficient in converting waste BTUs to methanol BTUs, and it does so at costs equivalent to gasoline production costs.[17] According to the same European Union study, the U.S. could produce 28 million tons of methanol per year from the pulp and paper industry alone. This is the thermal equivalent of .6 quads or 4.6 billion gallons of gasoline. Notice that the demand for transportation liquid fuels in the U.S. using PDHEVs would only be 1.2 quads or 10 billion gallons of liquid fuel (chart p. 12-13). In other

---

[16]57,000 BTUs per gallon for methanol compared to 115,000 for gasoline and 128,000 for diesel

[17]Institute for the Analysis of Global Security, www.iags.org, Tomas Ekblom study for the European Union from 12-'03.

words, waste from the pulp industry could supply almost half of all required personal transportation liquid fuel for the U.S.

As mentioned, methanol is currently produced using natural gas, but there are other places to get methane (natural gas) than from fossil fuel sources. One such place is municipal solid waste landfills where methane build up is a serious hazard, not only because it is explosive, but because it is twenty times more damaging than carbon dioxide as a greenhouse gas. There are 1300 landfill sites in the U.S., about 900 of which could be a source for methane, according to the Methanol Institute. According to William Wisbrock of Alcohol Solutions LLC of St. Louis, Missouri in his report, "Green Methanol From Landfill Gas," 1.6 billion gallons of methanol could be produced in the U.S. per year from landfill gas now either trapped or in the process of escaping into the atmosphere. The first commercial scale plant producing methanol from landfill gas is now in operation near Columbus, Ohio where they are producing 15,000 gallons of renewable methanol and 40 tons of liquid carbon dioxide per day from 3 million cubic feet of landfill gas. Production of methanol will continue for fifteen years after the landfill is closed.[18]

Another possibility is to produce methanol from coal using an environmentally clean process developed by Air Products, Inc. and Eastman Kodak Corporation. A pilot plant operation using this "liquid phase conversion" process was operated for seven years in Tennessee where they produced 300 tons per day of methanol and a total of 104 million gallons over the course of the project.

Another attractive feature of methanol is that is can be used directly in Direct Methanol Fuel Cells (DMFC) and high temperature fuel cells, such as Solid Oxide Fuel Cells (SOFC). Smaller versions for use in powering laptops, cell phones and other electronics will be commercialized in 2004. DMFC motorcycles will follow within a few years. The technology can be scaled up for use in DMFC powered automobiles. Methanol is an ideal hydrogen carrier containing 12% hydrogen by weight. In fact, on a volumetric basis, methanol is a better hydrogen carrier than hydrogen! The best weight percentage that can be obtained by compressing hydrogen gas is about 6%...and it requires energy to compress it, which lessens the overall efficiency of using this form of hydrogen.

---

[18]New Biomass-to-Methanol Process Could Compete For Tax Subsidies, March 19, 2003, www.fuelsandvehicles.com

Fisher-Tropsch Chemistry

Fisher-Tropsch is a chemical process used to make synthetic fuels such as gasoline or diesel fuel. It was developed by German chemist Franz Fisher (1852-1932) and Hans Tropsch (1839-1935) of Czechoslovakia in the early 1930s. The process was used successfully by Germany in WW-II to make motor fuel. The process uses hydrogen and carbon monoxide heated to 400^OF and passed over a nickel or cobalt catalyst to form a hydrocarbon mixture. Today, the country of South Africa makes 80% of their motor fuels this way with coal as the initial feedstock.

A low sulfur gasoline or diesel fuel can be made using Fisher-Tropsch chemistry for about 60-80 cents per gallon with no additional refining costs once the fuel is produced.

Ethylene synthesis

Even more economical than Fisher-Tropsch, recent research headed by Dr. George Olah at the Loker Hydrocarbon Research Institute at the University of Southern California has shown that methanol can be dehydrated to ethylene ($CH_2=CH_2$) using certain catalysts. Ethylene in turn can be made into gasoline or diesel fuel economically. The conclusion is that methanol could become the feedstock for diesel equivalent fuels.[19]

Mobil-M Process

In the 1980s Mobil Oil Company developed a special zeolite catalyst, which enabled them to convert methanol into gasoline. Zeolites are silicate minerals that have cavities and pore dimensions that can selectively produce hydrocarbon molecules within a desired size range, in this case carbon chains of about eight atoms long.

The process proved to be viable but was discontinued in the 1990s after only a few years of operation when the price of oil dropped back down to the ten dollar per barrel range. It could be that these types of liquefaction processes are once again worth looking at with the price of oil at $40 per barrel.[20]

---

[19]Ohlah, George. "The Methanol Economy," *Chemical and Engineering News*, 22 Sept 2003:5
[20]Probstein, Ronald F. and Hicks, Edwin. *Synthetic Fuels*, McGraw Hill 1982, p. 277-79.

Gas To Liquid Processes

Biomass gasification is a thermochemical process, whereby a carbon rich organic material, such as wood, rice hulls, or corn stover, is heated in an updraft or a fluidized bed gasifier. The hot product gas consists of methane, carbon monoxide, carbon dioxide and nitrogen where the methane is usually used to fire an on site process or for heating. Since the methane produced this way has a production cost of over $4 per million BTUs, the success of this type of operation is highly dependent on the price of natural gas. New developments use a reactor that increases the methane production making biomass gasification once again a potentially viable method of producing combustion gases and also hydrogen.

Anaerobic digestion is a biochemical process utilizing microorganisms to break down biomass in an oxygen free environment producing methane and carbon dioxide. With reactors, the methane concentration can be as high as 90% and generally can be produced for under $4 per million BTUs.

The gaseous products of both the gasification and digestion processes can be liquefied with the use of catalysts to form liquid fuels, such as methanol and even synthetic oil. The cost for producing methanol this way is about 60 cents per gallon (equivalent to $1.40 gasoline), and the cost for synthetic oil is about $2.45 per gallon but expected to come down with increased interest in these processes.

Biocatalysis

The conversion from fossil fuels to an economy based on living plants depends upon the ability to use cellulosic biomass to make liquid fuels, such as methanol, ethanol or fuel oils.

The traditional method of producing ethanol from corn uses only the grain portion, the starch, of the plant. Research laboratories have now developed forms of bio-engineered catalysts (enzymes) that speed up the process of the conversion to alcohols from cellulosic biomass, which includes the stalk and formerly wasted part of the plant.[21]

---

[21]Cellulosic biomass generally refers to all of the plant matter including the stems and fiber as opposed to starch biomass, which is limited to the seeds and fruit of the plant. Starch readily converts to glucose which is used to make alcohols; cellulose is more difficult to break down into glucose.

Fast Pyrolysis

As with the TC process (see page 16), fast pyrolysis converts biomass, such as forestry waste, agricultural waste, rice husks, bagasse and corn stover directly into oil, carbon and non-condensable gases. The gases are used to fire the process in a bubbling fluidized bed reactor. The feedstock is heated to 900oF without oxygen where it vaporizes into gases and char (carbon). The char is removed and the gases are cooled quickly to condense into oil. No waste is produced in this process, patented by DynaMotive Corp. of Vancouver, Canada. A 200 ton per day plant built in West Lorne, Ontario will produce 200,000 barrels of competitively priced oil per year which can be used directly in a gas turbine or non-turbocharged diesel engines. The fuel production cost, including debt retirement, is 78 cents per gallon of diesel equivalent fuel.[22]

The fast pyrolysis thermal conversion process will typically convert biomass to oil at 75% efficiency; one ton of biomass will yield two barrels of petroleum equivalent energy content oil.

---

[22]According to a report of Octagon Capital Corporation, Toronto, Canada, authored by John A. Clarke 19 July 2004.

2 Basic Energy Concepts

ENERGY

Energy can be neither created nor destroyed, but it can be made to change forms. Some forms of energy are more "user friendly" than others; they are more socially useful than others, and hence, have more value. The fact that there are issues of "value" suggests that there are important economic considerations as well as political and social considerations that are now part of an overall fundamental understanding of energy.

This chapter looks at the different forms in which energy is found, and how it is stored, released and converted from one form to another. We will also consider some concepts that are related to energy in peripheral ways, such as the idea of sustainability. The concept of the commons is important because all people need intact, functional ecosystems, oceans and a viable atmosphere -- systems that are truly global.

Another related concept examined here is that of "accountability." In economic terms, it means figuring the costs associated with energy conversion, and just as importantly, the costs usually *left out* of the accounting process, called externalities.

Primary Energy

Primary Energy is energy as it is found in nature, the bulk forms of raw energy that enter our society on a tanker or a freight train, for example. Primary energy usually needs to be converted into forms of energy that the consumer can handle and use.

Primary energy now enters the U.S. economy as either a fossil fuel or as uranium ore for eventual use in nuclear power plants. The useful forms of energy that we purchase as consumers to power our vehicles and appliances, heat our homes and give us hot bath water originated as a form of primary energy.

Pimary energy is differentiated into two classes, representing the core thesis of this book. The two classes are:

non-renewable, primary energy sources, such as coal, crude oil and uranium ore, that are acquired, extracted, used and the waste discarded.

renewable energy, such as biomass and wind, that are recycled continually within the ecosystem being renewed after use by incoming radiant energy from the sun.

Non-renewable energy systems are considered dirty because the primary energy is only used once and the end products, such as carbon dioxide (CO_2), ash, mercury and uranium ore are then discarded into the environment as waste.

Renewable energy is considered clean because essentially there is no waste. All end products are reused with energy being transformed, not used up (see Figure 2.1). Transitioning energy systems from the non-renewable "old way" to the renewable "new way" represents an energy "Power Shift"...a fundamental change in the way we think about energy.

End Use Energy

End use energy refers to forms of energy and fuels that can be easily stored, transported, purchased locally and used safely by the average consumer. Discussed are four forms of useful energy: fuel oil and methanol (liquid fuels), electricity and hydrogen. All four forms are energy carriers and must be made from primary energy.

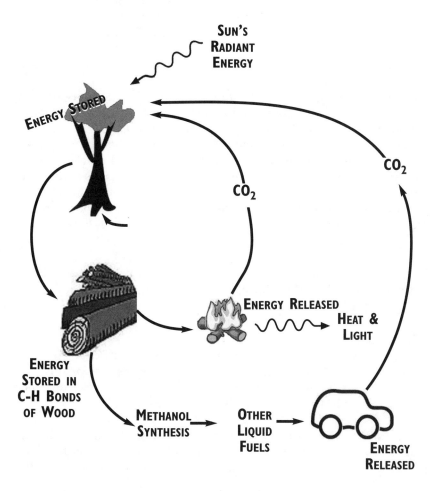

SUN'S
RADIANT
ENERGY

ENERGY STORED

CO_2

CO_2

ENERGY RELEASED

HEAT &
LIGHT

ENERGY
STORED IN
C-H BONDS
OF WOOD

METHANOL
SYNTHESIS

OTHER
LIQUID
FUELS

ENERGY
RELEASED

SUSTAINABLE ENERGY USE

FIGURE 2.1

Liquid fuel

Liquid fuels are generally easy to store and transport and they have a high "volumetric energy content," which simply means that a lot of energy can be stored in a small volume. The characteristics of liquid fuels were discussed in the previous chapter. Traditionally we have used gasoline and diesel fuel, but these fossil fuels can be replaced with a clean liquid fuel oil product that can be made from depolymerized waste and biomass.

Methanol is another form of liquid fuel that is easy to transport and store but with only about one half the volumetric energy content of gasoline. It has other desirable properties, however, and that may be enough to overcome the volumetric energy content shortcoming. It can be converted to other liquid fuels, such as gasoline which has a higher energy content, and it can be used directly in several kinds of fuel cells (Direct Methanol Fuel Cells and Solid Oxide Fuel Cells). In addition, methanol can be made from waste and biomass, landfill gas or flared gas at oil wells that is now wasted.

Electricity

The most versatile of the energy carriers, but whose primary draw-backs are that it is difficult to store and is transported long distances only with difficulty.

Hydrogen

In many ways, hydrogen is the ideal energy carrier: it's clean, in that it contains no carbon, and it's safe because it disperses so readily if it escapes from its container. It is not clean, however, if it is made either directly or indirectly from fossil fuels or nuclear power.

The emphasis in this book is on energy carriers other than hydrogen because some of the formidable obstacles in implementing the much ballyhooed hydrogen economy are yet to be overcome, which we'll discuss in more detail under hydrogen physics (page 79).

There are formidable obstacles regarding both the physical properties of hydrogen as well as the politics regarding the implementation of any new energy scenarios. There are those who do not want to see a departure from our current, highly profitable, fossil fuel based economy. For the next 10-20 years, it is still possible for some corporations to make a lot of money on the massive consumption of fossil fuels.

WHERE ENERGY IS FOUND

There are four places where energy potential is found: chemical bonds, the moving mass of air or water, radioisotope fission (see page 73) and the sun's radiation. This potential can be captured or released...and used for our benefit.

Energy stored in chemical bonds

Hydrocarbons, as the name implies, contain hydrogen and carbon atoms joined together with covalent chemical bonds. In any plant matter, these bonds represent energy, originally from sunlight, but now stored as carbon-hydrogen bonds or carbon-oxygen bonds. To a lesser degree nitrogen, sulfur and other trace mineral atoms are also involved.

For example, in a campfire, the energy in the chemical bonds of the fuel (wood, which is a carbohydrate) can be released as heat and light in the process of combustion. The C-H and C-O bonds have the same energy content whether they are three months old (plant matter biomass such as wood) or 300 million years old (fossil fuels such as coal).

The storage and release of chemical energy

In the case of biomass or fossil fuels, the sequestering of energy occurs when photons, the sun's radiant energy, are transformed by the process of photosynthesis into the chemical energy of the covalent bonds in living matter. Photosynthesis is the natural process by which green plants convert water and carbon dioxide into carbohydrates and oxygen.

Discussed here are two processes by which energy is stored: photosynthesis (Figure 2.2) and electrolysis (Figure 2.3), and two processes by which energy is released: combustion (Figure 2.4) and the fuel cell (Figure 2.5).

STORING ENERGY

PHOTOSYNTHESIS

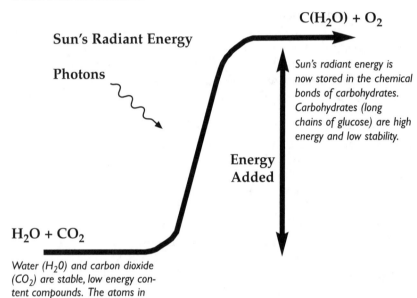

$C(H_2O) + O_2$

Sun's Radiant Energy

Photons

Sun's radiant energy is now stored in the chemical bonds of carbohydrates. Carbohydrates (long chains of glucose) are high energy and low stability.

Energy Added

$H_2O + CO_2$

Water (H_2O) and carbon dioxide (CO_2) are stable, low energy content compounds. The atoms in these molecules are in very stable bonding arrangements.

FIGURE 2.2 Under the right conditions and with the proper catalysts and energy input, here in the form of photons from the sunlight, the stable bonding arrangements found in H_2O and CO_2 are broken. The O-H (oxygen-hydrogen) bonds in water are stable but low energy. The newly formed C-H (carbon-hydrogen) bonds in the carbohydrate are high energy (low stability). Indeed, the sun's energy is now stored in the chemical bonds of the plant matter. Carbohydrates now become an energy carrier. Over long periods of time, heat and pressure applied to carbohydrates form hydrocarbons (crude oil for example) which also carry energy.

STORING ENERGY

ELECTROLYSIS

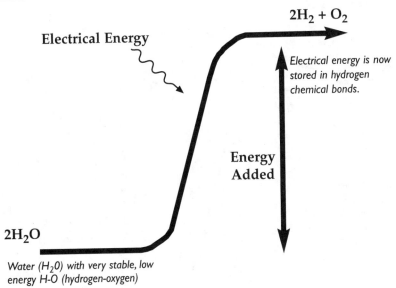

$2H_2 + O_2$

Electrical Energy

Electrical energy is now stored in hydrogen chemical bonds.

Energy Added

$2H_2O$

Water (H_2O) with very stable, low energy H-O (hydrogen-oxygen) bonds.

FIGURE 2.3 Electrical energy (direct current) is conducted through the water. This added energy breaks the stable H-O (hydrogen-oxygen) bonds of the water molecules. New higher energy (although less stable) bonds are formed as hydrogen (H-H) and oxygen (O-O) gas. Hydrogen now becomes an energy carrier with the energy from the DC electricity carried in the H-H (hydrogen-hydrogen) bond.

RELEASING ENERGY

COMBUSTION

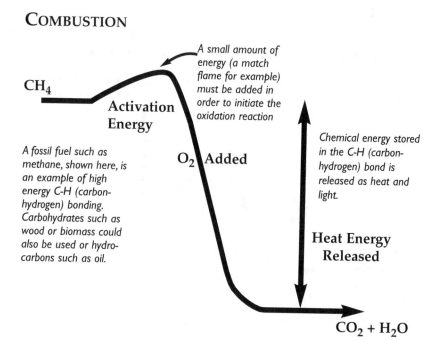

CH_4

Activation Energy

A small amount of energy (a match flame for example) must be added in order to initiate the oxidation reaction

A fossil fuel such as methane, shown here, is an example of high energy C-H (carbon-hydrogen) bonding. Carbohydrates such as wood or biomass could also be used or hydro-carbons such as oil.

O_2 **Added**

Chemical energy stored in the C-H (carbon-hydrogen) bond is released as heat and light.

Heat Energy Released

$CO_2 + H_2O$

FIGURE 2.4 The O_2 molecule (the oxidant) accepts electrons in this reaction and is "reduced" chemically. At this point energy is released from the C-H (carbon-hydrogen) bonds of the methane. New, lower energy (but more stable) compounds such as CO_2 (carbon dioxide) and H_2O (water) are formed as the reaction products.

RELEASING ENERGY

HYDROGEN FUEL CELL

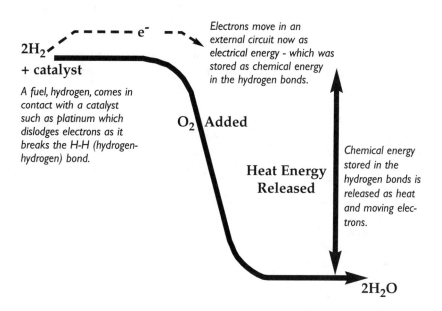

2H₂ + catalyst

A fuel, hydrogen, comes in contact with a catalyst such as platinum which dislodges electrons as it breaks the H-H (hydrogen-hydrogen) bond.

Electrons move in an external circuit now as electrical energy - which was stored as chemical energy in the hydrogen bonds.

O₂ Added

Heat Energy Released

Chemical energy stored in the hydrogen bonds is released as heat and moving electrons.

2H₂O

FIGURE 2.5 The oxidant, oxygen, accepts the electrons in an electrochemical reaction (not combustion). This releases heat energy as the high energy oxygen bonds are broken and reformed into lower energy (but more stable) bonds in water.

ENERGY STORED IN A MOVING MASS

Wind

Wind is a good example of energy stored in a moving mass, air which is set in motion by the uneven heating of the earth's atmosphere. This energy source is properly considered solar energy because, ultimately, it was the sun's radiant heat that caused the air to move. Other examples of a moving mass that may be tapped for energy include ocean currents and ocean waves. Again, the ultimate source of this energy is the sun.

The amount of potential energy in the wind is enormous and can best be described in terms of how much can be practically extracted with present day wind generators.

There are ten states that each have wind resources from which over a trillion kWh per year of electrical energy could be practically extracted. Compare the total residential demand for the U.S. now at about 1.2 trillion kWh with what is available from just seven of these states.

> Kansas has 1.6 trillion kWh
> Texas has 1.6 trillion kWh
> North Dakota has 1.5 trillion kWh
> Nebraska has 1.3 trillion kWh
> South Dakota has 1.2 trillion kWh
> Oklahoma has 1 trillion kWh
> Montana has 1 trillion kWh
>
> 7 State Total = 9.2 trillion kWh

This wind energy potential is taken from a U.S. PIRG report done in 2003.[1] These data do not take into account a Stanford University study, done about the same time, which concluded that the wind potential is actually 24% greater than previously thought because of the higher hub height and greater efficiency of the larger units now being used.

---

[1] Wind data as published in the USPIRG Education Fund Report 2003 which can be read in full at www.pirg.org. PIRG credits the Union of Concerned Scientists for the data which includes areas of class three and greater, land areas only within 20 miles of existing transmission lines, excluding all urban area, excluding all environmentally sensitive area, 50% of forested areas, excluding 30% of agricultural land and excluding 10% of all range land.

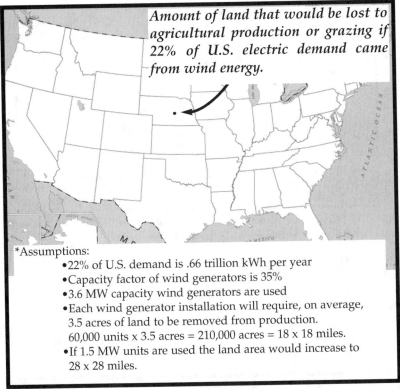

Amount of land that would be lost to agricultural production or grazing if 22% of U.S. electric demand came from wind energy.

*Assumptions:
- 22% of U.S. demand is .66 trillion kWh per year
- Capacity factor of wind generators is 35%
- 3.6 MW capacity wind generators are used
- Each wind generator installation will require, on average, 3.5 acres of land to be removed from production.
  60,000 units x 3.5 acres = 210,000 acres = 18 x 18 miles.
- If 1.5 MW units are used the land area would increase to 28 x 28 miles.

FIGURE 2.6 illustrates the enormous amount of energy contained in moving air. The little square shows an area 18 miles x 18 miles; this is the amount of land that would be required to actually accommodate the wind generators and access roads to them for 22% of the U.S. electrical demand to be furnished with wind. In actual practice, the wind generators would be dispersed, with most of the land around them used as it was before the generators were put in place.

Ocean Waves and Currents

Ocean wave motion and ocean currents represent another example of a mass in motion from which energy can be extracted. Since waves and currents are the result of winds blowing across wide expanses of ocean surface and the ocean's absorption and release of energy from the sun, they should rightfully be considered solar energy.

Average wave power of greater than 15 kWh/meter has the potential to generate electricity at competitive prices. Wave energy along both the east and west coasts of the U.S. is typically in the 20-30 kW/meter range.

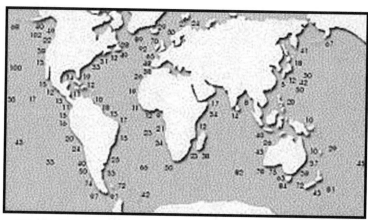

Figure 2.7 World wave resource map from Ocean Power Delivery Ltd. shows the average wave power in kilowatts per meter of wave crest.

Wave energy conversion systems have been developed in the U.K. where there is sufficient wave front energy on the U.K. shoreline to power the country three times over. At this time, the economically recoverable wave energy resource for the U.K. is about 25% of current demand, about 87 billion Wh/year.[2] . A wave energy conversion system occupying one square mile and placed off the U.S. west coast would supply electricity for over three million homes.

FIGURE 2.8 To illustrate the enormous amount of energy in moving water, consider the Gulf Stream. At 50 miles wide by 200 feet deep and moving at 3.4 mph, it contains so much kinetic energy that if the energy in the cross sectional area at any one point could be captured, it would, theoretically, be the equivalent of hundreds of full sized nuclear power plants. Of course, all the energy could not come close to being captured, but some of it may soon be with the Florida Hydro Power & Light project described in Chapter 1.

---

[2]Ocean Power Delivery Ltd. July 2004 <www.oceanpd.com>

The density of ocean water is 832 times that of air, making the kinetic energy available from a 5-knot (5.75 mph) current equivalent to a wind velocity of 168 mph. For the same cross sectional area, a turbine in an ocean current would produce about 180 times as much power as a wind generator.[3]

One of the strongest ocean currents, the Gulf Stream, flows adjacent to the densely populated east coast of the U.S. (Figure 2.8), and contains enough energy to supply the northeast U.S. The Florida Hydro Power and Light project is the first to take advantage of the energy from the Gulf Stream. As discussed in Chapter One, other ocean current projects are underway in San Francisco Bay and New York City.

Radioisotope Fission
Some naturally occurring atoms decay into other atomic forms giving off heat, sub-atomic particles and radiation in the process. There are ways to accelerate this natural fission process and harness the heat, which is given off in large quantities. Nuclear reactors, for the generation of electricity, is the example which probably comes to mind at first but geothermal energy is also a way of harnessing the heat given off by the decay of certain radioactive elements. Harnessing geothermal energy is possible when the naturally occurring radioactive decay is taking place relatively close to the surface of the earth, as is the case in fourteen or so western states.

Solar Energy
Almost all of the energy we use (except nuclear and tidal currents) ultimately comes from the sun...including fossil fuels. As a resource, the sun's energy is practically unlimited; the question is how to capture it for direct use since it is so dispersed.

In the U.S., the annual average solar radiation reaching the surface of the earth varies from about 135 kWh per square foot-year in the Pacific Northwest and the Northeast to about 213 kWh per square foot-year in the sunny Southwest. A reasonable average for the country would be about 170 kWh per square foot-year or 580,000 BTU per square foot-year. There are three ways that this energy can be captured: passively, with building design features that allow for the capture of solar energy within the building; with solar thermal systems, which allow for the capture of solar energy with collectors; and with photovoltaics (PV), the direct conversion of the sun's energy to electricity.

---

[3]Blue Energy Canada, Inc. July 2004 <www.bluenergy.com>

THE CONVERSION OF PRIMARY ENERGY TO USEFUL FORMS OF ENERGY

In any conversion process, some energy is always lost. The question becomes, what are the implications of the energy loss when one considers the overall operation of the system compared to the value added in the process.

There are three things to consider with energy conversion processes:
1. The input into the system in either BTUs or in dollars (cost)
2. The output from the system in either BTUs or dollars (value)
3. The conversion device itself in terms of its associated costs

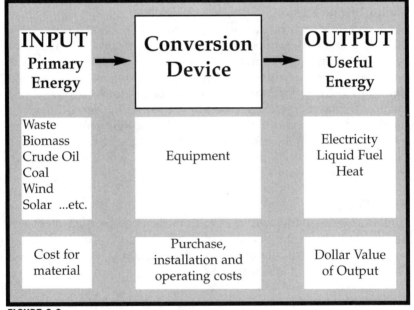

FIGURE 2.9

The output divided by the input will give an idea of the efficiency of the system, especially when all input costs and energy values are considered.

Using net output, the value of the output minus the value of the input (net output) over the life of the system, we can compare one system to another in terms of life cycle costs. This calculation can also be described as a kind of net energy analysis (NEA).

Efficiency is a measure of energy waste in a system, that is energy lost in the conversion process. When primary energy (energy in an unusable form) is converted into useful energy, this can be thought of as energy recovery. There may be less total energy content in the output form, but it's useable and, hence, more valuable.

Volumetric Energy Content

The limiting factor often is the available space in which to store the energy we will be using. For example, a typical automobile gas tank has about 2.7 cubic feet of volume, and that is about all of the space that

Cost of Energy			
Energy Source	Volumetric BTU Content	Cost of the Energy	Cost in Dollars per million BTUs
Electricity [3412 BTU/kWh]		$.07 per kWh	$20.00
Propane	93,500 BTU/gal	$1.16 to $1.63 per gallon	$12.40 to $12.50
Hydrogen [61,000 BTU/lb]	780 BTU/ft³	$2 per kg	$17.50
Gasoline	115,000 BTU/gal	$1.75 per gallon	$12.50
No. 2 Fuel Oil Diesel	128,400 BTU/gal	$1.75 per gallon	$12.50
Fuel Ethanol	76,000 BTU/gal	$1.00 per gallon	$11.00
Methanol	56,800 BTU/gal	$.50 per gallon (whs)	$7.73
Natural Gas, Retail	1000 BTU/ft³	$6 per million BTUs	$6.00
Natural Gas, Wholesale	1000 BTU/ft³	$3.50 per million BTUs	$3.50
Wood [8,000 BTU/lb]	200,000 BTU/ft³	$100 per cord	$4.00
Coal,anthracite [25 mil.BTU/ton]		$25 per ton delivered	$1.00
Coal		$6 per ton at mine	$0.24

FIGURE 2.10

is allowable for a passenger car. The more energy we can get into the 2.7 cubic feet the better, and the further we will be able to go.

One of the characteristics of "useful" energy is that it is in a form that is energy dense, meaning a lot of energy in a small volume or high volumetric energy content. It is easy then to compare fuels, especially liquid fuels, based upon how much energy they have for the same volume. See Figure 2.9.

Conservation and Efficiency
Same energy services but with less input
An important premise of this book is that as alternative ways of acquiring and using energy are examined, the end use benefit of the energy still remains the same. In other words, the end use benefit of a freezer is that it keeps two hundred pounds of food at minus 10°F. The "usefulness" of the electrical energy is simply keeping the 200 pounds of food at minus 10°F. The end use benefit of an SUV is that it enables the owner to go 15,000 or 20,000 miles per year in a certain amount of luxury and carrying the whole soccer team not just the balls. The end use benefit of space heat is that our living space remains at 72°F all winter. As considered in this book, conservation and efficiency measures should not affect the end use benefits.

Efficiency refers to a "technological" fix, an improvement in a device that converts energy so the device is able to use less energy to accomplish the same outcome as before. Conservation generally refers to a change in lifestyle that enables one to enjoy the same end use with less energy input. In either case, we are not suggesting that it is necessary to "freeze in the dark" in order to accomplish the social goals that use energy and make our lives comfortable. Conservation and efficiency measures only affect the amount of energy required as input into the system...the output remains the same.

Conservation and Efficiency as a Way of Acquiring Energy
Saving a certain amount of energy is the same as acquiring that same amount of energy. Assume that there are two paths to the exact same result in terms of a social good, say a hot bath. One path is very inefficient; suppose the tub is missing the plug and hot water is continually exiting down the drain. The other, more efficient, path involves a "technical fix" in the form of a $1.00 plug. In fact, a great deal of energy is conserved with this latter path. The constant in this case is the hot bath; it can be maintained by purchasing more energy to make more

hot water for let's say $200 over the course of time, or a plug can be purchased for $1. The latter choice avoids the purchase of $199 worth of natural gas; the baths are all the same. The latter choice is equivalent to the purchase of $199 worth of natural gas and yet it only cost one dollar. To avoid the cost of primary energy and yet retain the same or greater benefit is equivalent to actually acquiring this difference in energy. After all, it's the benefit we are concerned with, not the primary energy itself.

National energy policy has a lot to say about how primary energy is acquired, what emphasis and funding conservation and efficiency measures will receive, and what effort will be devoted to the new technologies that will enable the society to function more efficiently. The later chapters of this book will look at some of these issues in detail.

DISTRIBUTED GENERATION (DG)

Making Electricity on Site
Distributed generation means producing electricity at the site or near the point of use instead of at a large centralized power plant many miles away from the end user.

There are compelling reasons why distributed generation has advantages over centralized power generation. Several obvious reasons are listed below. In their comprehensive and powerful study, *Small is Profitable*, The Rocky Mountain Institute sites no less than two hundred and seven well documented and supported benefits of distributed generation.

Modular
Distributed generation (DG) equipment is smaller sized and modular so with thousands of power generation units all the same, it becomes easier to fund and build the same generating capacity as compared to one huge central plant. For the same reasons, it is also much quicker time wise, and there is less financial risk.

Heat Recovery
When using high temperature fuel cells, the power source is on site so heat can be recovered and used for space heating, domestic hot water or industrial process heat.

Less cost
Distributed generation costs less. The assumed economies of scale do not apply; it actually costs more per kilowatt of delivered power from a large central plant than it would cost from distributed generation. This is especially true when full cost accounting is applied and externalities are taken into account.

Better quality power
The quality of the generated electricity is better for distributed generation and there is less power loss.

More reliable power
The reliability of the power is better with distributed generation. For critical uses, such as the computer industry, financial centers, data centers, etc., there is less down time with distributed generation.

Cleaner, more efficient
DG is much cleaner environmentally as well as more energy efficient.

More secure
National security is enhanced with distributed generation because of the decentralization; there are no centralized targets that would make large segments of the system vulnerable.

Creates more jobs
Distributed generation creates more jobs; it is better for local economies as well as the national balance of payments.

Does away with the grid
Distributed generation makes it possible to do away with the grid. On average in the U.S., it costs 2.4 cents per kWh, one third of the retail rate, just to deliver the electricity via the grid. It costs more to deliver it than it does to generate it.

Certainly, there may be some instances where large centralized generation is preferable, but in general, the country would see great benefits from distributed generation. There are no insurmountable technical or practical barriers in moving to a distributed generation system; the barriers are largely institutional, political and bureaucratic.

SOME HYDROGEN PHYSICS

This book focuses on replacing non-renewable and nuclear sources of primary energy with forms that are renewable. The energy carriers would continue to be electricity and liquid fuels; the difference is that they would be produced cleanly and with renewable primary energy. Hydrogen is being discussed widely as a revolutionary new and clean form of energy, but it has some problems associated with it that need to be addressed long before the so-called hydrogen economy becomes a reality.

Hydrogen itself is perfectly clean; when combined with oxygen in a fuel cell it produces electricity with hot water being the only by-product.

Hydrogen is not a naturally occurring fuel; it is an energy carrier that has to be produced. Not only does it have to be produced, but it also has to be stored, transported and handled by the consumer...safely and conveniently, to say nothing of inexpensively.

An ideal energy carrier would have minimal problems associated with its production, storage, transport and end use...not so with hydrogen.

Despite the fact that it gives up its stored energy very cleanly, the main difficulties with attempting a hydrogen economy in the near future are centered around production and storage, assuming that the technical hurdles can be overcome regarding hydrogen fuel cell durability and cost.

Production of end use fuels should be inexpensive, clean and done locally with minimal externalities, but this is not necessarily so with hydrogen. The production of hydrogen may not be such a clean process with the current administration which is advocating coal and nuclear energy to make it...a truly self-defeating proposition. If hydrogen is not made with clean renewable energy resources (wind, waste, biomass and sun), there is no point in even considering a hydrogen economy, unless it's a political smoke screen for another agenda.

Storage should be trouble free, and it should be easy to transport, preferably, a liquid fuel which is easy to pump and transfer. Good storage characteristics also imply a high volumetric energy content...but this is not so with hydrogen.

Storage of hydrogen is problematic because it is a very light gas. Hydrogen has a high energy content by weight, BTUs per pound or BTUs per kilogram, in fact hydrogen has about three times more energy by weight than gasoline. A gallon of gasoline weighs about three kilograms and there is about the same energy in a kilogram of hydrogen as a gallon of gasoline. The problem is that getting a kilogram of hydrogen in a relatively small volume, say the same volume as a gallon of gasoline, is not easy. If hydrogen gas is compressed to 10,000 PSI (about the maximum possible), it would still occupy three times the volume required for one gallon of gasoline.

These same volumetric constraints on the storage of hydrogen also affect the ability to transport bulk hydrogen over long distances economically. Instead of trucking, it may be possible to pipe hydrogen, but that has its own set of problems and expenses.

End use should be easy for the consumer -- non-toxic, liquid, low cost and safe. High volumetric energy content means that the fuel needs to be handled less often and takes up less space in the vehicle, which is problematic with hydrogen gas.

End use friendliness would be hampered by the fact that it would be stored onboard at 10,000 PSI. Some people may have a disinclination to sit so close to a tank under such extreme pressure.

Each of the above areas are being researched and there are promising developments, but there is also a long way to go.

The premise of this book is that, instead of hydrogen as an energy carrier, it is possible to use technologies that are available now, or at least very close to commercialization, to solve our energy related problems. Everything that needs to be done can be done today with no wait and no temptation to use dirty sources of primary energy.

SOME RELATED CONCEPTS

Sustainability

A sustainable system is one that can continue to operate indefinitely, without end. If a system is sustainable, it means that future generations will have the opportunity to do exactly what we are doing today. In this book we are thinking in terms of energy conversion systems, but it makes no difference what kind of system is under discussion...if one generation uses it up for their own benefit leaving an altered or degraded state for those in the future, their behavior can be described as unsustainable. A few concepts associated with the notion of sustainability will help to define why some systems, or patterns of behavior, are sustainable and some are not.

A linear system starts in one place, moves in a line to another point, and stops. It has a beginning and an end...it is not sustainable. It can be done once and it results in a change in form that cannot be reversed or repeated exactly.

The use of fossil fuels is a good example of a linear system. There is a finite supply (cannot be renewed), it moves in one direction to an end point (carbon is transferred from below ground to the atmosphere), where the process stops.

At some point, one part of the system or the other runs out of capacity; either the fuel runs out or the atmosphere runs out of holding capacity to absorb the carbon...eventually something must give. Also note that because it is linear, it can only be done once. Future generations will not have the same opportunity.

Contrast the linear system to the cyclic system where there is no beginning and no end. It continues indefinitely with conversions continuously taking place, energy being exchanged and matter transformed, but the system itself continues forever.

An example would be the life cycle of carbohydrates (plant matter). The continuous input of sunlight keeps the cycle going in the same way, generation after generation.

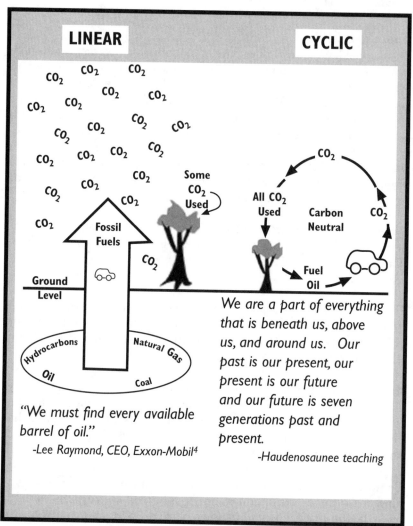

FIGURE 2.11 In the linear system, the carbon-hydrogen bonds (in the form of oil, coal and natural gas) are "mined" and then the carbon is dumped into the atmosphere where it builds up. In the cyclic system, the carbon-hydrogen bonds are continually recycled within the atmosphere and ecosystem. There is no build up of carbon in the atmosphere.

[4]Cambridge Energy Association Conference Speech, 12 February 2003.

Capital and Income
Money in the bank is "capital, " and if left there, it will produce income at a certain rate of interest. Seeds can also be considered capital; they can be used to produce more plants, which in turn will replenish the original seeds. The crop can be considered "interest" and can be consumed or sold minus enough seeds to continue producing a crop. If the seeds are not replenished, that is if the system is not sustained, then the result is starvation.

The money in the bank could be considered economic capital, the seeds could be considered natural capital, remembering that in each case the interest can be spent but the capital must remain in place…it cannot be used up or the system will collapse.

Now consider the case of fossil fuels, such as oil or natural gas. These fossil fuels are a form of capital; they are fixed and in place and may be able to produce some dividends, maybe not. The point is that they are capital…but are treated by traditional economists as though they are interest, and so we are "spending" them as though there was, literally, no tomorrow. The same traditional economists, who are disregarding the concept of sustainability, and the principle of exponential growth (Figure 2.11), are treating capital as though it was interest.

The Myth of "Sustainable Growth"
By definition, expansion and continuous unrelenting growth are not sustainable. There are always limits to growth; in the case of cancer, the patient dies. In the case of overburdening the natural ecosystems of the earth, we see collapse. Yet in the case of economic systems, we see traditional economists and policy makers insisting that growth is good, implying that growth is sustainable.

The operative concept here is the "exponential" characteristic of economic growth; it is not linear, it is exponential. A 5% per year growth rate, for example, means that each new year's growth is based upon the previous year, and that upon the year before, and so on. It means that the rate itself accelerates, as an exponential function not as a linear function. The implications of exponential growth are truly staggering. It should be obvious that systems that demonstrate exponential growth, such as global population, energy use and consumption must be put into a dynamic equilibrium before the limits to such growth are reached, or the consequences would be catastrophic. Doing this, however, would require that societies take into account the welfare of future generations.

The energy systems described in Chapters One and Six are sustainable; those discussed in chapter three are not sustainable.

Exponential Growth

When newscasters, politicians and economists talk about economic growth, they mean exponential growth -- as opposed to linear growth. For example, a 5% growth rate means that after this year's growth of 5%, the *new total* next year then expands another 5%. The new total at the end of next year then grows at 5% the following year, and so on. The rate is compounded year after year just as interest in the bank is compounded. This is an example of "exponential" growth, and it is profoundly different from linear growth. Populations and economies exhibit exponential growth, as does consumption when it is based on either populations or economies growing at certain percentage growth rates.

As a way to illustrate exponential growth, consider the growth of two trees. Tree "A" grows in a linear fashion, as do all trees, let's say at a rate of 1/8" (tree ring width) per year. Tree "B" will grow normally for the first ten years at which point it will begin to grow exponentially, let's say at a rate of 10% increase per year. We'll let the trees grow for 250 years which is about seven generations. At the end of ten years, Tree A and Tree B are both 2 1/2" in diameter (1/8" x 10 x 2). At the end of 250 years, Tree A is 5 feet in diameter (1/8" x 250 x 2). Tree B's growth will be compounded at a rate of 10% for the last 240 years. Let's see what the difference in the diameter is as a result of the 10% per year *increase* in growth compared to the constant (linear) growth of Tree A.

The diameter of Tree B is calculated as follows: $(1.10)^{240}$ = 8.6 billion x 1/8" x 2 (growth in year 10) = 2.15 billion inches = 33,913 miles in diameter which is more than four times the diameter of the earth.

A typical Chinese dynasty was about 500 years duration. The preclassical Mayan period was 2,000 years duration. What if they or the Chinese expected a 5% economic growth rate? Yet prominent economists and policy makers today are suggesting that our economy should expand at a compound rate of 5%; that it would be good for business. It goes without saying that the implications for future generations of compound growth is suicidal.

The Concept of the Commons

"They hang the man and flog the woman
Who steals the goose from off the common.
But let the greater villain loose
Who steals the common from the goose."

Anonymous, Poem from medieval times.

Commons are joint use lands (or water) where local groups of people are all permitted to use the land "in common." There is no individual ownership and all have rights to the common property. Most people are familiar with the medieval village meadow where all of the peasants had land use rights to graze their sheep. By agreement the villagers would only use half the meadowlands in a given year, allowing the other half to lie fallow. It was the commons that was the basis for their independence and self-sufficiency. The commons allowed for at least an element of variety and richness in the humble peasants' lives.

The commons represents natural life support systems. Examples of commons today would include oceans, fisheries, sustainable old growth forest, wild rivers, the air itself, wilderness expanses, fresh water lakes and aquifers. Should they be kept intact and shared sustainably? Should they be exploited by certain privileged small groups who profit immensely while others are left out?

"We must find new lands from which we can easily obtain
raw materials and at the same time exploit the cheap slave
labor that is available from the natives of the colonies. The
colonies would also supply a dumping ground for the surplus
goods produced in our factories."

Cecil Rhodes, "founder" of Rhodesia

Expropriating the commons is called "enclosure" and is usually characterized as economic progress by those doing the expropriating. Those who are losing their ancestral lands or waters, of course, don't see it that way; for them it's a devastating loss of their security, sustenance and independence. So called economic progress for a few often results in the displaced people ending up on a human scrap heap as economic slaves to another foreign system. The hallmarks of enclosure are always short-term economic strategies that are not sustainable.

The economic strategies outlined in chapter six are intended to be an honest way to evaluate ideas in terms of sustainability by taking into account all people affected, including future generations.

Externalities
Full cost accounting
Full cost accounting means adding everything up as opposed to adding up only what one chooses to add up, perhaps "forgetting" some things (externalities) that are inconvenient to think about.

Externalities are those costs that somehow just don't quite make it onto the official accounting tally. They are, as the term implies, external. They are not accounted for in one place, but they are paid for in another because all costs must be paid. If there were "full cost accounting," that would not be the case, but there is not a full accounting when reporting many of the costs associated with primary energy and the conversion of primary energy to useful energy.

Coal is notoriously cheap, about $6 a ton to take out of the ground and about $24 a ton delivered to the power plant a thousand miles away from the mine. When the cost of electricity is figured, it is based on the $24 per ton to purchase the coal but may not include other costs associated with the coal, such as the release of mercury to the atmosphere when the coal is burned. Airborne mercury finds its way into the lakes where it is converted to methyl mercury in the lake bed. The methyl mercury then works it way up the food chain to the large sport fish, such as walleyes.

Consumption of mercury, which is a dangerous neurotoxin, is problematical. In fact, the state of Minnesota has found mercury contamination in virtually all of its famous 10,000 lakes. The Minnesota Department of Natural Resources is compelled to issue fish advisories for all of the fishing lakes in order to protect the health of those who eat the fish; pregnant women are advised to never eat the fish. Minnesota, a state which relies heavily on the sport fishing tourist dollar, has a serious and very real problem. The cost, in any event, is external to the $24 per ton cost of the delivered coal, and yet someone does have to pay for it. It just is not included in the cost of the electricity. Deciding how the externality is accounted for is based largely upon political influence. The person with neurological damage from eating mercury laden fish probably has very little political influence; the tourism and sport fishing industry whose income is threatened probably has a bit more influence, but not as much as the power company that is burning the coal.

Lobbying against a utility is a truly humbling experience with, in the case of Minnesota, a utility lobbyist for each couple of legislators. The externalities get paid, but not by the utility; they get pushed onto society as a whole as with all externalities.

An even more egregious example is the nuclear industry, which has managed to avoid the cost of decommissioning the power plants after they have served their useful life (about thirty years). The bill for cleaning up the mess may easily reach $400 billion. Without this $400 billion external cost, nuclear generated electricity is already a loser in the marketplace, and this is before we even consider the terrorist threat to nuclear plants and the vulnerability of outside temporary storage of spent nuclear material at the plant sites.

Externalities are those costs that are not figured in as they would have to be if there was full cost accounting, as there is with your home budget or the way your business must be run. Most of us don't have the luxury of ignoring some costs and paying only selected others. We must pay all of the costs that we incur in our personal lives. Many of the external costs are those that large industries have not just forgotten about, they are costs that the industries have arranged to have excluded from the balance sheet. Externalities are also costs that large industries do not want you to know about. Why? Because we are paying for them; because these costs have been pushed onto society at large to pay for. This sleight of hand can only be accomplished when the public is unaware of it or their attention has been diverted. As you will see, there is a huge difference between the reported cost of energy and the true cost of that same energy.

Although they are not counted in the reported cost of energy, externalities are paid for by someone at sometime. By leaving these costs out of the energy accounting process, some forms of energy appear to be cheaper than they really are. Externalities can be difficult to quantify but that does not mean that they do not exist. They can be acknowledged and discussed even though there may not be a dollar figure to accompany them, or, the cost can be estimated so at least we get an idea of their magnitude. Chapter Three is devoted almost entirely to externalities, and we will see that many of the difficult to compute human and environmental costs are simply left out of the equation altogether. One such example is global warming.

Global Warming Basics

The global warming basics are quite simple: When carbon dioxide and methane, and chlorofluorocarbons (CFCs), the principle greenhouse gases, build up in the atmosphere, the blanket of gases and air trap the sun's energy and proceed to heat up...a so called "greenhouse effect" takes place.

What mankind has done over the past 200 years of the industrial age is, in a linear fashion, move massive quantities of carbon from beneath the ground, where it had been for hundreds of millions of years, to the atmosphere. The carbon dioxide level has now reached a record level of 379 parts per million (ppm), the highest it has been in 400,000 years (see Figure 2.12, 2.13 and 2.14). This year about seven billion more tons of carbon will be put into the atmosphere of the earth, a behavior that is clearly not sustainable.

Three entities (the oil industry, the U.S. Government and the insurance industry) cannot afford to deny the evidence of global warming, and, therefore, consider it a reality. Contrast that approach with an approach where the denial of the reality of global warming allows one

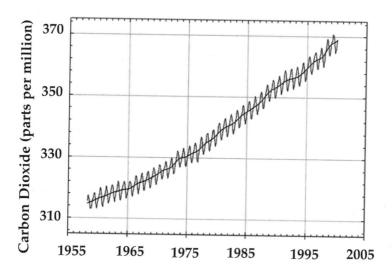

FIGURE 2.12 Atmospheric carbon dioxide concentrations measured at Mauna Loa Observatory in Hawaii over the past 50 years. National Oceanic & Atmospheric Administration (NOAA) Climate Monitoring & Diagnostic Lab. www.cmdl.noaa.gov

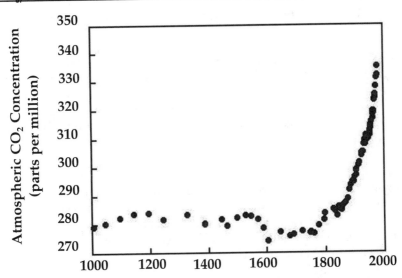

FIGURE 2.13 Atmospheric carbon dioxide concentrations over the past 1000 years up to 2000. The most recent data from March, 2004 shows carbon dioxide levels at 379 ppm. **Plot that point on the graph above.** **NOAA Paleoclimatology** Program. www.ngdc.noaa.gov/paleo/paleo.htm

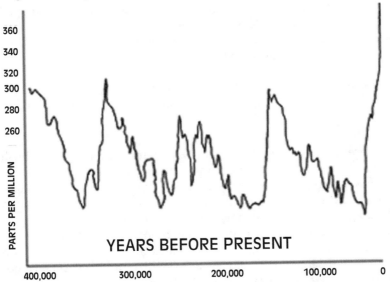

FIGURE 2.14 Atmospheric carbon dioxide concentrations over the past 400,000 years. Notice the almost vertical rise in the curve at present and notice that 370 ppm exceeds all levels of atmospheric CO_2 in the past 400,000 years. Prehistoric CO_2 levels are determined by ice core samples taken in Greenland and the Antarctic. **NOAA Paleoclimatology Program and UK Climate Research Institute.**

to continue to profit from the transfer of carbon from below ground into the atmosphere.

Royal Dutch Shell Oil, the Pentagon and the insurance industry (page 91) cannot afford to deny the evidence of global warming and, therefore, consider it a reality. Contrast that approach with an approach where the denial of the reality of global warming allows one to continue to profit from the transfer of carbon from below ground into the atmosphere.

The Oil Industry

Royal Dutch Shell Oil Company has already spent $32 million per offshore oil rig to raise each one six feet higher above the ocean surface. The reason for this expensive corporate decision is because of the threat of more extreme weather and higher sea levels as a result of, you guessed it...global warming.[5]

Oil companies can explore for oil and operate on the Arctic tundra only when roads are frozen solid with a foot of ice and a six inch snow covering. These conditions are established by Alaska Department of Natural Resources rules. In 1970 they were able to operate 200 days a year; by 2003, the number of days that they could operate had dropped to 103 according to Alaska state documents. If oil companies cannot operate for 120 days or so per year with consistency, they cannot successfully explore and develop the area.

In June 2003, the U.S. Department of Energy appropriated $270,000 to help Alaska rewrite its rules governing how thick ice roads need to be.

The U.S. Government

The recent Pentagon study that was suppressed by the Bush Administration from the time it was written in October 2003 until it was leaked to the *Observer* in the U.K. and published in February 2004, warns that because of impending severe climate change the Pentagon is making military plans for a planet on the edge of anarchy. The report is entitled "An Abrupt Climate Change Scenario and its Implications for United States National Security" states that as early as 2010 we could find ourselves in the midst of a destabilized and devastated global ecosystem because of rapid climate change.

---

[5]"Greenhouse Effect: Shell Anticipates a Sea Change." *New York Times*,12 December 1989.

The Insurance Industry

The largest re-insurance company in the world, Munich Re, the second largest re-insurance company in the world, Swiss Re, Lloyds of London and sixty-nine other insurance companies from twenty-five countries have signed and released a document that expresses their view of global warming and climate change.   The document is entitled "A Statement of Environmental Commitment by the Insurance industry." The insurance companies are concerned all right. As stated by Munich Re over ten years ago, they are concerned that human induced climate change will bankrupt the industry. The insurance industry has also stated that they must change the way they calculate their risk; they can no longer base the actuarial tables on the incidence of past natural events.   Insurance companies are now listening quite seriously to atmospheric scientists and their views regarding a destabilized atmosphere (see Figure 2.15)

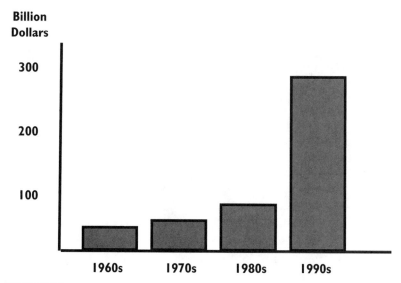

Weather Catastrophe Related Costs To The Insurance Industry

FIGURE 2.15

3 The Old Way of Acquiring Energy

COAL, NUCLEAR AND FOREIGN OIL

We will look at three major sources for primary energy: coal, nuclear and foreign oil. Associated with these three sources of energy are eighteen factors that we ask the reader to consider; factors which bear upon job creation and local economies, factors which bear upon balance of trade and the national economy, factors which affect the environment and factors which bear upon our national security. Keep in mind also that associated with these forms of primary energy are many external costs or externalities. Again, these external costs are not generally reflected in balance sheets; they are hidden, but none the less they are borne by society at large. The costs are socialized (borne by the society at large) while the profits are privatized (kept by corporate interests). The eighteen factors listed and discussed here are only touched upon and most could easily be a separate book.

For hundreds of years, whale oil lamps were used for lighting, in which case whale oil would be considered as primary energy. Even today, hardwood forests are decimated in order to make charcoal which is used for heat and for cooking in much of the developing world. We can easily see why whale oil and hardwood charcoal are inappropriate fuels. Coal, nuclear and oil could also be considered inappropriate fuels, fuels which represent outmoded and problematic ways of acquiring primary energy.

ELECTRICITY FROM COAL

In the U.S., the majority (approaching 60%) of our electricity comes from coal fired central power plants. Worldwide, coal now provides 23% of all energy and is in decline; in 1910, for example, 62% of the world's energy was derived from coal. The industrial revolution 150 years ago was based on coal as an energy source; it has always been relatively accessible and relatively cheap, but coal is the most carbon laden of all the fossil fuels with up to 98% carbon content. This has grave implications for global warming in a world where CO_2 levels are the highest they have been in 420,000 years and making our planet's surface the warmest it has been in 1200 years.[1]

There are six factors, in addition to global warming, to think about when considering the merits and perils of obtaining electricity from coal fired power plants. This section will give a glimpse of some factors associated with taking the coal out of the ground and some factors to consider regarding human health, not only in mining the coal but in breathing the air pollutants after the coal is burned. We will look at the coal fired power plant in some detail because there are more factors to consider here as to whether or not the continued use of coal is the best approach to our energy needs. Once the electricity is generated, it must be distributed with large grid networks that are the source of most of the maintenance problems as well as a host of other problems, including cost. We then take a look at cleaning up the mess; the air pollution, the methyl mercury in the lakes, and coal bed methane as a more recent phenomenon. Lastly, this section deals with the subsidies and giveaways to the coal industry and suggests that there may be a better place to put our tax dollar.

For each of the six factors below, the reader is asked to consider the "externalities" associated with that particular factor.

1. Mining the Coal

In the United States about 60% of our electricity is generated in coal fired power plants. We have plenty of coal, about a 400 year supply at current consumption rates, and it's cheap at $24-$32 per ton delivered to the power plant. Operations that can locate at the mine can purchase coal for as little as $6 per ton. Coal mining regions in West Virginia,

---

[1]Dun, Seth, "King Coal's Weakening Grip on Power."*World Watch* Sept-Oct 1999:15.

THE OLD WAY OF ACQUIRING ENERGY
EIGHTEEN FACTORS TO CONSIDER

Electricity from Coal	Electricity from Nuclear	Gasoline from Foreign Oil
1...Acquisition Mining coal	7...Acquisition Mining Uranium	13...Acquisition Military involvement Environmental damage at wellhead -- flaring, spills
2...Health factors Black lung Particulates Asthma Mercury	8...Health factors Refining uranium Contamination at the refinery and mine	14...Pipelines Human rights factors Use of local military to protect pipelines
3...Power plant Wasted energy costs to install the plant	9...Power plant Costs to install the plant	15...Shipping Tanker wrecks Bunker crude
4...Transmission lines The "grid"	10...Terrorism Plutonium and U-235 to weapons Plants as a target	16...Terrorism Embargoes, Price instability
5...Cleaning up the Mess Mercury Reclamation of strip mines Other air pollution, acid rain, carbon dioxide	11...Cleaning up the Mess Decommissioning, reclamation of mines Nuclear waste disposal	12..Cleaning up the Mess Reclamation Air pollution, flaring Global warming Associated toxins
6...Subsidies and giveaways Coal gasification "clean" coal	12...Subsidies and giveaways "Stranded costs" Price-Anderson Loan guarantees	18...Subsidies and giveaways Billions and Billions of Dollars to oil corporations

FIGURE 3.1

Virginia, Pennsylvania, Ohio, Illinois, Indiana, Kentucky and Alabama produce most of the 990 million tons of coal used per year in the U.S, with Montana and Wyoming producing minor amounts. There are two methods of extracting coal from the ground; strip mining from the surface and underground mining, both methods having severe environmental impacts. In strip mining, gigantic power shovels scoop overlying soil and rock to get to the coal seam that could be as much as one hundred feet below the surface, creating obvious environmental destruction in the process. This is the least expensive method of extracting coal. The other method, underground mining, requires shafts that penetrate far underground to the coal seams as well as human labor to dig and load the coal. In addition to the environmental damage, there is a large human price that has been paid over the years with this method of extraction...cave-ins, injuries, black lung disease and the exploitation of labor pools in depressed areas of the country.

The mining process itself, in addition to burning the coal, releases 25 million tons of methane annually, a potent greenhouse gas that has the global warming impact of the entire carbon production of the U.K.[2]

2. Health and Human Issues
Black Lung
Pneumoconiosis (black lung disease), a debilitating decline in lung function caused by the inhalation of coal dust, has been under-reported, concealed by coal company doctors and misdiagnosed for the past 60 years. Lawmakers had to be forced by the largest strike in U.S. history to enact compensatory and preventative measures, and U.S. taxpayers have paid out more than $30 billion to compensate mining families.[3] This money is an externality, an expense that is certainly paid for but it is not included in the cost of coal or the cost of electricity from the coal fired electrical power plants. The journal *Science* reported on a study that found that the cost of coal-generated electricity would be 50% to 100% greater if these externalities were included.[4]

According to the National Black Lung Association, 1500 former miners a year die of black lung disease.[5] The Federal Black Lung Benefits Act

---

[2]Dunn,Seth, "King Coal's Weakening." *World Watch*. Sept/Oct 1999:16

[3]Derickson, Alan. "Black Lung: Anatomy of a Public Health Disaster" *World Watch* Sept/Oct 1999: 14

[4]Jacobson, M.Z. and Mastes G.M. "Exploiting Wind versus Coal" *Science* Aug 24, 2001:.1438.

[5]Nixon, Ron. "Waiting to Exhale: New Federal Rules Could Help Coal Miners Breathe Easier" *Mother Jones*. Jan/Feb 2001: 21.

was set up in 1969 to provide benefits to miners who suffer from the disease, but federal figures show that less than 6% of the claims filed are honored; coal companies have lobbied and fought the miners' claims saying that "it is an assault on profitability." According to the US Department of Labor, nearly half of all mines have submitted false reports to conceal hazards including dangerous levels of coal dust.

Jobs
Decreasing employment: At one time the U.S. coal industry employed over 700,000 miners, today there are fewer than 80,000 miners because of greater mechanization and the trend toward surface strip mining. Both the U.K. and China are experiencing similar drops in mining workforces and are planning solar-cell manufacturing sites in the effected mining areas in an effort to ease the transition for workers.

Transporting the Coal
Most coal is transported by train which itself burns fuel oil but is also a source of "fugitive dust" from open railroad cars. For example, the coal fired power plants in Minnesota and Wisconsin obtain their supply from Montana, North Dakota and Wyoming. A typical power plant burns about 8000 tons of coal per day, it would require a train one mile long to transport this amount of coal.

3. The Power Plant
About a fourth of all primary energy used in the U.S. (24 quads) is in the form of coal, which is used to fire centralized electrical generation plants...plants that in turn waste two thirds of it as lost heat.

The 8000 tons of coal per day will fire a typical 1000 megawatt (MW) power plant. The coal is burned to produce steam under high pressure that turns the steam generator producing electricity. This one plant will produce 800 tons of boiler residue per day and 800 tons of fly ash per day that must then be disposed of in landfills. In addition, the plant will release 20,000 tons of global warming carbon dioxide and another 800 tons of sulfur dioxide to the atmosphere. The plant may have scrubbers to remove some of the sulfur dioxide, but don't bet on it. The new U.S. energy policy (May 17, 2001), and lobbying by the Bush administration on pending energy legislation through 2003, recommends easing this type of requirement for power plants.

The efficiency at which electrical energy is converted from coal energy is about 35% for the typical power plant. In other words 65% of the stored energy in the form of carbon- hydrogen bonds within the fossil fuel is lost...wasted, and along with the waste are the pollutants of course.

4. Transmission Lines

The Rocky Mountain Institute (*Small is Profitable* p.78, 213-220) calculates that it costs, as a national average, about 2.4 cents per kWh in expenses associated with the electrical grid just to transport and distribute the power to the consumer, in addition to the fact that transmission lines lose from 7% to 10% of the energy in transit. About 90% of the maintenance and operational costs for central plant electricity are associated with the grid. Transporting the electrical energy in high voltage transmission power lines has its own set of problems, as 50 million electricity consumers in the Northeast and parts of Canada found out on August 14, 2003 when they lost power.

As discussed in Chapter Two and as Amory Lovins demonstrates so convincingly in his 390 page treatise, *Small is Profitable*, with 207 reasons, distributed generation makes a lot more sense than high voltage, expensive and trouble prone grids.[6]

5. Cleaning up the mess
Mercury
Mercury in the coal is vaporized in the combustion process and later absorbed in falling rain only to end up in the waterways and lakes. Minnesota, the land of 10,000 lakes, cannot identify one of the 10,000 that is not contaminated with methyl-mercury. Methyl mercury, the organic complex of elemental mercury, tends to bio-accumulate in the food chain making the fish unsafe to eat and requiring the state Department of Natural Resources to issue advisories regarding the poisoned fish for all fishing lakes in the state. You will recall that Minnesota relies heavily on its tourism and sport fishing industry for income into the state.

Mercury, a nerve poison, breaks down proteins in both plants and humans; chronic exposure in humans leads to permanent brain damage. Fifty per cent to seventy five per cent of all airborne mercury can be attributed to human activity, specifically the burning of coal.[7]

---

[6]Lovins, Amory B. *"Small is Profitable"* Snowmass: Rocky Mountain Institute 2002 p108 and inside cover recap of 207 benefits of distributed resources.

[7]Bright, Chris. "Mercury Pollution May Dwarf Published Levels," *World Watch*. Mar/Apr 1995: 6.

Respiratory Disease

Historical attempts to curb the ill effects of burning coal go back to 1306 in London.[8] Prolonged inhalation has been linked to a large range of respiratory and cardio-vascular problems as well as cancer and high infant mortality rates.[9]

Mine Reclamation

Strip mining (photo below) results in just about total ecological destruction, which is extremely difficult to reclaim even if the means and the will to do it are present. With adequate water, of which the west is lacking, it would take decades for the original landscape to be restored. In the mean time erosion and acid leaching from the waste heaps have an adverse effect on the surroundings, especially streams and rivers.

Air Pollution

Pollution from coal plants is a global problem. Atmospheric scientist Thomas Cahill of the University of California at Davis reports evidence that Chinese coal fired power plant airborne pollution is blowing all the way across the Pacific ocean and fallout containing nickel, copper, lead, zinc and arsenic is being found as far east as the Rocky Mountains.

---

[8] Dunn, Seth. "King Coal's Weakening." *World Watch*. Sept/Oct 1999: 13.
[9] Dunn 13.

Carbon dioxide: Although all fossil fuels release carbon dioxide into the air, coal releases more than the other fossil fuels, 78% more than natural gas for example. The limiting factor then in terms of global greenhouse gases is the amount of atmosphere we have to absorb it all, not the reserves of fossil fuel left to exploit. It makes no difference how large the reserve of fossil fuel is if we have destabilized the atmosphere of the earth to the point of potential major catastrophe.

Acid rain: Carried aloft, usually with the help of giant smokestacks, sulfur dioxide and nitrogen oxides form acids that return to earth damaging buildings, soils, rivers, lakes and crops. It is thought that by 2020 sulfur emissions in China resulting in acid rain will overwhelm fertile soils across not only China but also Japan and South Korea.[10]

Germany is taking a lead in renewable energy technology and a possible reason may be the almost universal awareness of the German citizens to the situation in the Black Forest, which is considered to be a national treasure of Germany. The Black Forest is dying. In some areas, people have painted a desperate plea on some of the trees: "hilf uns" which means "help us,"...help us indeed. The cause of its impending death is not contested; it is acid rain. It is known that rainfall is acidified by atmospheric pollution as a result of coal burning central power plants and other industrial processes, but the chemistry is rather complex. Nitric acid and sulfuric acid are formed in the atmosphere when coal and petroleum are burned, but this is complicated by other chemical pathways equally devastating, such as the interaction of unburned hydrocarbons and atmospheric moisture. The result is the dying off of entire forest ecosystems in central Europe causing great concern among the Germans as well as other people in the region.

In Sweden, a similar catastrophe is taking place, this time with the lakes being acidified with acid rain runoff that is percolating through soils that lack calcium carbonate (limestone) that has the ability to neutralize the acid rain. Four thousand lakes in western Sweden are now biologically dead with another 14,000 in serious decline. These lakes have no life except a kind of filimentatious algae that has taken the place of the complex natural life systems in the lakes. There has been an attempt to remediate some lakes by airlifting large amounts of carbonate onto the lake surface and, thereby, neutralize the acid water. It has worked pretty well except the cost is $50,000 per lake per year and it must be done continuously, year in and year out.

---

[10] Dunn 15.

A similar phenomenon is occurring in the Adirondack Mountains in upstate New York in the U.S. where 20 lakes are now dead with another 200 in serious decline. For example, the last trout caught in Woods Lake was in 1969; the birds have now disappeared from the area and even the frogs are now gone. The lake is dead.

Other parts of the eastern seaboard of the U.S are also affected where the rain is now about ten times more acidic than it was just a few dozen years ago. In Camels Hump, Vermont, the red spruce started dying off at high elevations about fifteen years ago. There were many theories, but no one knew for sure what was happening. After considerable research, it is now known that the mix of hydrocarbons and nitrous oxides in the upper atmosphere are leaching valuable minerals, primarily magnesium, from the foliage of the trees. Eventually the trees die under the onslaught, in some areas of the Great Smoky Mountains 95% of the red spruce are now dead.[11]

Ozone: Each year ozone costs the U.S. between $5 and $10 billion in crop losses. Wheat yields in parts of China have been cut by 10% because of ozone alone.

Global Warming

The implications of global warming are far greater than simply the "slight" increase in average air temperatures that we hear reported in the news. Global warming means unintended, unforeseen consequences; it means a destabilized atmosphere...not one that is simply a few degrees warmer. For example, World Health Organization (WHO) epidemiologists indicate that climate change would change the range of many diseases which are now constrained geographically by the distribution of their host species.[12]

Those who think they can profit in the short term by ignoring the indicators of climate change often cite professed skeptics of global warming. On the other hand, the $1.4 trillion insurance industry, which must make important investment decisions based upon the likelihood of future climatic disasters, takes the prospect of their own financial risk, and global warming, very seriously.[13]

---

11 Acid Raid, New Bad News. Videocassette. Auth. Alexander Scourby, WBGH TV, Boston, Mass. Time-Life Video. (MLA) 58 min.

12Wilken, Elena. "Tropical Disease in a Changing Climate." *World Watch.* Jan/Feb 1995: 8-9.

13Flavin, Christopher. "Storm Warnings: Climate Change Hits The Insurance Industry." *World Watch.* Nov/Dec 1994: 12-13.

The misconception that many have regarding global warming is that they think the only consequence is the warming of the earth's air temperature by a few degrees. The problem is that this warming, even just by a few degrees, affects the atmospheric and oceanic systems that regulate the world's weather.

According to the EPA, there is more carbon in the atmosphere now than anytime in the past 400,000 years, primarily as a result of two human activities; burning of fossil fuels and destruction of the world's forest ecosystems.[14] The study notes that old growth forests absorb four times as much carbon as plantation and newly seeded trees despite what the forest industry claims. Industrial tree planting does not prevent global warming, in fact it may help speed up the process.[15]

A new hydrologic study[16] shows that the amount of fresh water flowing into the Arctic from Eurasia's six largest rivers has increased in precise proportion to Arctic increases in surface air temperatures (global warming). This phenomenon has the potential to upset the existing undersea currents in the Arctic that now bring much warmer deep waters to the surface, thereby warming the adjacent land masses. In this case, global warming could cause regional cooling, an unexpected consequence.[17]

The Inuit live in precarious balance with the Arctic ecosystem and serve as the "canary in the mine" -- a warning to the rest of the world as to what's in store in the near future if global warming is not stopped. Measurements indicate that in recent years, the summertime ice thickness has thinned by 40% in the high Arctic with serious consequences for the Inuit people. Increasingly, their summer camps are being cut off by slush, cached meat is thawing and rotting, igloos that are losing insulating properties because of thaw and refreeze cycles, permafrost is melting and lakes are draining into the sea, and early ice breakup is carrying seals out of reach. What happens in this region could have a direct influence on global weather patterns. More warming, cloudier skies and higher sea levels are only a hint of other unintended consequences.

Tuvalu is an isolated island nation located between Hawaii and Australia in the Pacific Ocean with 11,000 inhabitants. Impending ris-

[14] Williams, Adam T. "Paper and Global Warming." *Earth Island Journal*. Summer 1998: 27.

[15] Williams 27.

[16]Stokstad, Erik. "River Flow Could Derail Crucial Ocean Current." *Science*. Dec 13, 2002: 2100.

[17]"Rivers Run To It." *Science News*. Jan 11, 2003: 29.

ing ocean levels caused by global warming threaten to destroy this small nation. This brings up the question of "ecological debt" where it should be decided if rich, environmentally irresponsible nations should pay for the loss of whole cultures, traditions and economies such as that of the Tuvalu's. We may find out if Koala Talake, Prime Minister of Tuvalu, has his way. He plans to take his case to the International Court of Justice in The Hague, Netherlands.[18]

6. Subsidies

Pending energy legislation (September 2004) gives $50 billion to the oil, gas and coal industries as an outright giveaway. The energy policy of the current Bush administration is to use more coal, spend more money on coal gasification and relax the pollution control standards for all of these industries, including emissions at coal fired power plants.

The big advantage of coal? It's cheap, or at least apparently so. Because of subsidies and external costs being shifted to the society at large, we are deceived into thinking that coal is cheap, abundant and irreplaceable. A European Commission study found that in a German coal fired generation plant, the cost of energy would rise by 50% if the externalized costs were borne by the power producer.

World Bank

The Institute for Policy Studies in Washington DC found that between 1992 and 1998 the World Bank gave $13.6 billion for the development of fossil fuel-fired power plants, coal mines and oil fields in developing nations. Seventy one of the 87 projects studied funneled money to corporations, such as Shell, Exxon and Westinghouse, where less than 9% of the rural poor people benefited from the funding.[19]

ELECTRICITY FROM NUCLEAR

When influential and powerful nuclear corporate interests are on the line, no matter how dismal a marketplace failure, the issue of taxpayer subsidies has a way of not dying. The underlying problem with nuclear, of course, is the fact that there is much more than an "energy" issue at stake here. Nuclear power generation is a legal way to make the weapons ingredient plutonium...this fact alone has tremendous political implications.

---

[18]Ede, Piers Moore. "That Sinking Feeling." *Earth Island Journal*. Winter 2003: 39. Also see www.climatesolutions.org

[19]Dunn, Seth. "King Coal's Weakening." *World Watch*. Sept/Oct 1999: back cover.

In general, there are three areas of concern regarding nuclear energy:

- There is the technology factor -- is it a beneficial way to generate energy from an engineering and technological point of view?
- There is the economic factor -- can it compete with other options in the marketplace?
- There is the human factor -- are humans capable enough and responsible enough to be entrusted with this technology?

The reader must answer those questions for himself or herself. In 1959, pro-nuclear scientists claimed that a nuclear fusion plant would be a reality in about 25 years. (1959+25=1984). In 1994, 35 years and $10 billion later, and after a major technological advance at Princeton University, pro-nuclear scientists announced that nuclear fusion was only about 30 to 35 years away ...about 2029.

As with the previous section on coal, the reader is asked to consider six factors (7-12) associated with this particular method of producing electricity. Keep in mind that all a nuclear plant is really supposed to do is boil water. After consideration, some would think that attempting to control and contain a thermonuclear reaction is a rather dubious way to go about boiling water...to say nothing about nuclear proliferation and cleaning up the mess.

7. Mining

Seventy-five thousand tons of uranium ore are mined per year to produce the 30 tons of enriched uranium required for each reactor. The residues or mill tailings left over from the extraction of uranium from ore, however, now amounts to 265 million tons of material, which litters the landscapes of the West. The citizens of Moab, Utah. have been complaining about a "humongous mound of uranium tailings" in their community for 25 years. The ten million ton tailings pile is leaching ammonia into the Colorado River and radioactive radon is continually wafting into the nearby city of Moab. The Department of Energy (you the taxpayer!) is considering moving the pile at a cost of $364 million.[20]

8. Health factors

American miners, as well as factory workers, in the enrichment and weapons industries risk getting cancer from exposure to radioactive elements.

---

[20]Long, Michael E. Half Life: The Lethal Legacy of America's Nuclear Waste." National Geographic. July, 2002: 28.

New Study from European Union

Research conducted by the European Committee of Radiation Risk (ECRR) suggests that previous studies published by the International Commission on Radiological Protection (ICRP), a group with close ties to the nuclear industry, have massively underestimated the impact of the nuclear industry on human life. According to the new study, pollution from the nuclear industry in the form of leaks associated with nuclear power plants and weapons testing will account for 65 million deaths in coming years. As a result of this research, there have been renewed calls in Europe for governments to discontinue support for the nuclear industry and to start thinking about accepting responsibility for the deaths and injury caused worldwide. This new study is thought to reflect more realistic risk assessment because of recent discoveries in radiation biology and human epidemiology.[21]

Nuclear reprocessing plants in La Hague, France, and Sellafield, England, have been and are continuing to discharge radioactive waste into the ocean with submerged pipelines according to reports from Greenpeace activists in Europe. Radioactive particles have been detected in sea life along the coasts of Scandinavia, Iceland, and into the Arctic. Although the practice is now banned, between 1950 and 1963 Britain dumped 28,500 barrels of radioactive waste into the Hurd deep off Cape de la Hauge in France.[22]

Sellafield soil tests

Scientists from the University of Bremen in Germany tested the soils near the Sellafield reprocessing plant in Britain and reported contamination levels equivalent to those around the ruptured Chernobyl plant in Russia. A British survey by George Know found increasing cancer deaths in children around the Sellafield and Dounreay nuclear facilities.[23]

Radiation effects near plants

According to a study conducted by the Radiation and Public Health Project in New York and reported on in the *Journal of Environmental Epidemiology and Toxicology*, 42 million people who live within 50 miles of and downwind from nuclear plants may be at increased risk of various types of cancer. The study also found that the Nuclear Regulatory Commission (NRC) has never voluntarily studied the link between

---

[21]Waugh, Paul. Deputy Political Editor. *The London Independent,* Jan 31, 2003.

[22]"Europe: Radioactive Dumping Via Pipe." *Earth Island Journal.* Winter 2000: 18.

[23]"Ebb and Flow." *Earth Island Journal.* Winter 1999: 3.

radioactive emissions from nuclear plants and patterns of cancer.[24] However, scientists in the Schleswig-Holstein area of Germany found that children living within 5 km of a nuclear plant were five times as likely to develop leukemia.[25]

A separate study, reported in the *Archives of Environmental Health*, examined infant death rates near five reactors, which "dropped immediately and dramatically" after the reactors closed.[26]

9. The Nuclear Power Plant

> *"The failure of the US Nuclear power program ranks as the largest managerial disaster in business history, a disaster on a monumental scale. The utility industry has already invested $215 billion (till 1985) in nuclear power, with an additional $140 billion to come before the end of the decade is out, and only the blind, or the or biased, can now think that most of the money has been well spent.   It is a defeat for the US consumer and for the competitiveness of the U.S. industry, for the utilities that undertook the program and for the private enterprise system that made it possible."*
>
> "Nuclear Follies," *Forbes* February, 1985,

In terms of the enriched uranium fuel, a nuclear plant operates at about a 3% efficiency rate, the other 97% being declared high-level nuclear waste looking for a repository.   Safety issues at the plants themselves are another matter and should also be considered carefully.

Davis-Besse (Toledo, Ohio)

> *"The closest brush with disaster since Three Mile Island."*
> Former Member of the Nuclear Regulatory Commission[27]

In November, 2001 the Nuclear Regulatory Commission (NRC) ordered the plant to be shut down for safety reasons and issued an order to that effect.   Incredibly the owner of the plant, First Energy

24 "Radiation and Public Health Project in New York," Journal of Environmental Epidemiology and Toxicology. Spring 2000.

25"Germany's Leukemia Cover Up." *Earth Island Journal.* Winter 1998: 3.

26Mangano, J.J., Gould, J.M., et al "Infant death and childhood cancer reductions after nuclear plant closings in the United States." *Archives of Environmental Health.* Jan/Feb 2002:

27Jackson, Hugh. "Atomic Economics." *In These Times.* Oct 14, 2002: 21.

Nuclear Operating Corporation, refused to do so and got the NRC to back down on their order.   Incidentally, this is the same First Energy that is involved in the blackout of August 14, 2003.   A few months later, in February, 2002 when the plant was shut down for scheduled refueling, a massive hole was discovered in a primary safety barrier, the reactor vessel head.   There was 3/8 of an inch of the six-inch thick stainless steel head separating them from a major catastrophe.   The Union of Concerned Scientists (UCS) and David Lochbaum the Nuclear Safety Engineer in the UCS Clean Energy Program were refused documents from the NRC in the course of their investigation.   Eventually, through the Freedom of Information Act (FOIA), the UCS was able to secure the documents and made them public through the UCS web site.[28]

Nuclear Plant First Cost

The Bush-Cheney energy plan, which proposes increased nuclear energy,[29] is based on a report prepared for the Department of Energy (DOE) by the Near Term Deployment Group (NTDG) composed of thirteen members.   Of the thirteen, at least ten are directly employed by the nuclear industry or have consulted for it.   This panel, of pro-nuclear industry corporate executives, estimates that new plants would cost $2,128 per installed kilowatt.   Some say the cost is actually much higher than that (exceeding $5000 per kW), but none the less, the well established cost for a gas fired plant is known to be $682 per kilowatt and they are getting cheaper to build all the time, now coming in at closer to $500 per kW.   The cost for wind is now figured at about $900 per installed kW.   Unable to avoid acknowledging the folly of nuclear plant construction, even the Bush administration states; "economic viability for a nuclear plant is difficult to demonstrate." So, what does the Bush blueprint call for in the 2003 budget request?   A $38.5 million subsidy to Dominion Energy, Entergy and Exelon to evaluate and get approval for sites where new nuclear plants could be built and $1.1 billion to build plants.   Incidentally, the NTGD report does not give consideration to renewable energy or conservation as an effective way to meet our energy needs.[30]

---

[28]"USC at Work: Successfully Seeking Documents." *Catalyst*. Fall 2002.

[29]400,000MW of new nuclear; Cray, Charlie. *Multinational Monitor*. Nov 2001: 12.

[30]Jackson, Hugh. "Atomic Economics." *In These Times*. Oct 14, 2002: 20.

10. Terrorism and Accidents

"It's a Brontosaurus that has had its spinal cord cut but is so big and has so many ganglia near the tail that it keeps thrashing around for years not knowing it's dead".

Amory Lovins, on the decline of the nuclear industry,
quoted in the Boston Globe, 1978

...that was 23 years ago and they are still thrashing around as of May, 2001 in the Cheney-Bush Energy Policy Report.[31]

The Nuclear Regulatory Commission's (NRC) response at a news conference in September, 2001 to a congressional allegation that their planning baseline did not take into account a hijacked airliner: "nuclear power plants are not designed to withstand such crashes."[32]

Decentralized energy sources are much less vulnerable to terrorist attack; terrorists probably are not interested in flying a plane into a photovoltaic panel or a wind generator. According to some knowledgeable sources, newer generations of nuclear plants are even more vulnerable than the older ones.[33]

A single major reactor accident would cost the country upwards of $400 billion plus hundreds of thousands of deaths. Such an incident could be caused by a single large commercial plane crashing into a containment building which in turn could cause a meltdown.[34]

After 15 years of congressional effort to increase nuclear plant security, the NRC agreed in 1994 to make provisions that would make it difficult to attack nuclear plants with truck bombs. The NRC also increased the number of security personnel and is, supposedly, doing better background checks for their employees.

Terrorism is not only an issue with the nuclear power plants; highly radioactive spent fuel rods must be transported cross-country from the plant to the disposal site, presumably Yucca Mountain, Nevada. A nuclear watchdog group in Wisconsin, Nukewatch, monitors this process by tracking and photographing such shipments. If this small,

---

[31]"Matters of Scale: Public Investment, Some Choices" *World Watch.* May/June 1994: 39.

[32]Cray, Charlie. "Too Cheap to Deter? The Nuclear Power Industry Pushes Ahead Post-9-ll." *Multinational Monitor.* Nov 2001: 13.

[33]Cray 16.

[34]Cray 13.

under-funded group can do that, then why couldn't a terrorist group target the shipments?

Exelon, a large nuclear operating company, proposed cutting nuclear power plant construction costs (which are at least three times the cost of a gas fired plant) by eliminating the containment structure on the so-called "pebble bed" type units.   That was before 9-11, they forgot to factor in the possibility of an attack by a civilian jet loaded with fuel. The pebble bed type units use graphite, which is highly flammable, as a matrix for the fuel pellets.   They walked away from the proposal after 9-11 and the NRC mothballed the idea.   Another close call?

Since 1991 the NRC has conducted numerous security tests where mock "intruders" attempt to penetrate the plant's security and disable the nuclear facility by simulating damage to the radioactive fuel.

Operational Safeguards Response Evaluation (OSRE) is an inspection program which simulates mock terrorist attacks on nuclear plants, it says a lot about the NRC's ability to evaluate nuclear plant security. After receiving advanced notification warning them of the exercises, 27 of 57 plants failed the test.   In 1998, the NRC's Office of Nuclear Reactor Regulation unilaterally and without notice to anyone terminated the program in an attempt to avoid further embarrassment.

According to studies done by the Union of Concerned Scientists who have been critical of the NRC procedures, the security measures at nuclear plants do not allow for more than one insider taking part in sabotage, they do not account for spent fuel being stored outside of the plant in far less secure conditions, nor do they take into account an attack by plane or truck.[35]

11. Cleaning Up The Mess

"Nuclear power, despite unprecedented and Herculean effort on the part of the nuclear industry, has died in the marketplace, a total failure.[36]

Cleaning up the mess refers to reclaiming the land and water degraded by uranium mines, decommissioning the nuclear power plants and dealing with problems associated with transporting and storing the 70,000 tons of highly radioactive waste in the U.S.

---

[35]Jason, Mark. "Overcoming Energy Insecurity." *Catalyst* Spring 2002: 4.
[36]Cook, J. "Nuclear Follies." *Forbes.* 11 Feb 1985: 85-87.

There are two main problems with radioactive waste: the first is that one has to find a place to store it, the second is the vulnerability to accidents and acts of terrorism during transport or while in storage.

The cost for decommissioning a nuclear power facility is estimated at $4 billion dollars per reactor. Included in the 1960s promise of "electricity too cheap to meter," we were told that future scientists would figure out how to deal with the waste. In 40 years, they haven't been able to do so. Perhaps until they do so, there should be a moratorium on building any new nuclear facilities.

Seventy-thousand tons of highly radioactive nuclear waste have to be shipped from nearly 100 power plant sites throughout the U.S. to a permanent repository where it needs to be stored safely for the next 100,000 years or so. The Bush administration says that Yucca Mountain Nevada will work just fine; we only have to transport the high level nuclear waste through 43 states within one mile of 52 million Americans. A single accident could easily cost between $10 and $14 billion to clean up. Yucca Mountain isn't even forecast by the Bush Administration to be ready until 2010 at which time it will still take 30-40 years, 80,000 truck and 13,000 rail shipments to accomplish the task.[37]

> *"We have found nothing so far that would disqualify the site...there are no show stoppers."*
>
> George W. Bush
> February 14, 2002

Some facts which come from U.S. government geologists: The Yucca Mountain site sits 12 miles from the epicenter of a 5.6 Richter scale quake that struck in 1992 and a 4.4 quake that struck in June, 2002. The site is between two active faults. The site is atop a major western aquifer and it is now known that the volcanic rock, which composes the site, is filled with tiny fissures that allow water to seep through it. It was later decided that the storage canisters should be fitted with titanium drip shields. Government engineers claim the storage casks are good for 270,000 years, but studies by Robert Loux of Nevada's Agency for Nuclear Projects says 500 years is more likely.[38]

---

[37]Smith, Gar. "A Gift To Terrorists." *Earth Island Journal.* Winter 2003: 42.
[38]Smith 42.

12. Subsidies and Giveaways

"economic viability for a nuclear plant is difficult to demonstrate."

Bush administration 2001

Despite the admitted inability to defend nuclear power on an economic basis[39] the Bush/Cheney energy plan of May, 2001 calls for much of the anticipated new generation of 400,000 MW to come from nuclear. As such, the Bush energy plan and resulting pending legislation (S-2095 for example) calls for continued massive giveaways to the nuclear industry.

Subsidies and giveaways come in at least five different forms and, according to U.S. Public Interest Research Group (USPIRG), amount to at least $10.5 billion per year. Estimates of giveaways to the nuclear industry add up to $146 billion not including the estimated $400 billion to decommission the existing plants and dispose of the high level nuclear waste. Here are some examples of how Congress is giving the nuclear industry a free ride.

Limited Liability Corporations (LLCs)

Bonding and insurance is a major expense for, say, a building contractor whose work or failure to perform or outright mistakes must be paid for when things go awry. The owners of nuclear power plants are allowed to form LLCs and, thereby, avoid the costs of adequate bonding or insurance which would hold them accountable to those who might suffer damage. The LLC allows companies to shield their assets while reaping maximum profits and amounts to a massive subsidy.[40]

Taxpayer Funded Insurance

There isn't an insurance company anywhere that would cover a nuclear power plant for liability (which says a great deal right there), therefore Congress, at the behest of corporate nuclear industry lobbyists, has shifted the liability to the taxpayer in the form of the Price-Anderson Act.

---

[39] Near Term Deployment Group Report: "A Roadmap To Deploy New Nuclear Power Plants in the United States as reported *In These Times*. Jackson, Hugh. "Atomic Economics" *In These Times*. 14 Oct 2002: 20.

[40] August 2000 study "Financial Insecurity: The Increased Use of Limited Liability Companies and Multi Tiered Holding Companies to Own Nuclear Power Plants" by Star Foundation and Riverkeeper. Mokhiber, Russell. "Nuclear Liability Shield." *Multinational Monitor.* Sept 2002: 30.

Without this exemption from liability in the event of a major catastrophe, even the advocates of nuclear power admit that they would be out of business. Price-Anderson is a subsidy of unknown but potentially gargantuan size, depending on the catastrophe. If a plant melts down[41] or is struck by terrorists, possibly more than $500 billion would be required to recover, according to a U.S government commissioned study carried out by Sandia National Labs. The value of the subsidy itself is estimated by the League of Conservation Voters to be worth up to $3.4 billion per year.

Furthermore, Price-Anderson indemnifies Energy Department contractors which means that any accidents at the contractor's facility or on the road is paid for by the taxpayer...including hauling the high level nuclear waste.

Price-Anderson is slated for renewal in current energy legislation.

Stranded Costs
Stranded costs are failed business enterprises where, instead of the developers taking the loss, the loss is shifted onto the taxpayer. Projects that are not economically viable, that is to say "losers", under normal conditions, would cost the promoters dearly. Even if written off as a tax liability, they are generally avoided because in the long run, losers don't result in viable, thriving business enterprises.

Stranded costs, on the other hand, are profitable for those who are positioned to cash in on them. After the so called "energy crises" in California in the 1990s, the stranded costs – that is power plants that were deemed to be unprofitable and were, therefore, "stranded" – came to $28 billion.[42]

The public, taxpayers and ratepayers have the cost shifted to them by means of state regulations while the energy corporations are not only let off the hook, but allowed to keep huge unearned profits. Stranded costs are a ripoff and are effectively a subsidy to energy developers.

---

[41]The outer surface of the Davis-Besse nuclear plant reactor core lacked a protective stainless steel cover. Over a 10-year period, boric acid routinely leaked onto it eating away 6" of carbon steel until it was 3/16" away from a meltdown. The plant's owner ignored numerous warnings over many years. Workers found it by chance while repairing a cracked control rod mechanism. *Davis-Besse: The Reactor with a Hole in its Head.* Union of Concerned Scientists. www.ucsusa.org fact sheet.

[42]Jackson, Hugh. "Atomic Economics." *In These Times.* Oct 14, 2002: 21.

Research and Development
Not including the $10 billion allocated for R&D in the current energy legislation, which is based on the Bush-Cheney energy plan of May, 2001, it is estimated that R&D money to the nuclear industry between 1948 and 2000 amounted to $65 billion.[43] The $65 billion, which is far less than the estimated $146 billion in all subsidies to nuclear, is in itself ten to fifteen times more than all R&D money directed toward fuel cell research in the past few years. High temperature fuel cells have the potential to supply far more electricity than nuclear plants and do it safely, at far less cost and without the electrical grid.

Decommissioning
The advocates, developers and promoters of nuclear energy have a tendency to forget to add in the costs associated with cleaning up their mess…decommissioning. This cost, which has to be paid by someone, is estimated at about $4 billion per plant.[44]

The external cost of decommissioning plants after their useful life of about 30 years is not part of the economic equation for the kW hour cost of electricity and is borne by the public at large.[45] The ability to avoid this huge expense is effectively a subsidy to the nuclear industry which could amount to as much as $400 billion.

Legislation now before Congress (May 2004) appropriates $1 billion for decommissioning nuclear plants.

GASOLINE FROM FOREIGN OIL

As with electricity from nuclear and electricity from coal, we ask the reader to consider six factors (13-18) which are associated with the pursuit of foreign oil and the use of petroleum for our transportation needs. In addition to keeping in mind the externalities associated with fossil fuels, consider the fact that the U.S. **does not actually need a drop of foreign oil**, not a drop. Some of the associated costs are politically charged and the subject of much debate, which illustrates the point that energy issues permeate our lives.

---

[43]Nash, Betty Joyce. "Mature Nuclear Plants Power District." Federal Reserve Bank of Richmond Regional Focus. Fall 2001. www.rich.frb.org/pubs/regionfocus/fall01/nuclear.htm.

[44]Long, Michael E. "Half Life: The Lethal Legacy of America's Nuclear Waste." National Geographic. July 2002: 9.

[45]Mokhiber, Russell. "Nuclear Liability Shield." Multinational Monitor. Sep 2002: 30.

13. Acquisition and Military Protection

This section considers oil exploration, drilling and flaring at the well-head as well as the use of military forces to acquire and protect the oil fields.

The connection between oil and the military is not a great mystery, they are two of the three largest industries in the world; military and weapons expenditures at $800 billion, illicit drugs at $500 billion and oil at $450 billion.[46] Acquiring oil and maintaining control over the reserves of oil is an important consideration for some governments, and it is not without consequences.

Local military forces are also used to protect oil pipelines around the world, but pipelines have their own set of factors to consider and are treated separately, in section 14, below.

The Caspian

The Caspian region generally refers to Kazakhstan, Azerbaijan, Uzbekistan and Turkmenistan, which together contain an estimated 150 billion barrels of oil and 14 trillion cubic meters of natural gas -- $2 trillion worth of oil alone.   That's $2,000 billion, and there is a gigantic scramble for a cut of the action on the part of corrupt, dictatorial regional government officials and on the part of the oil corporations developing the projects.   As usual, the people, the environment, human rights and democracy are left pretty much out in the cold.   Whenever that kind of money flows into a region, it has a destabilizing effect with a proliferation of military and arms and a greater divide than ever between those that are in a position to participate in procuring the resource and those without power.

A recent announcement (October, 2003) was made to the effect that 15,000 US troops were being moved into the Baku region of Azerbaijan to help combat "terrorism." Exploiting Caspian area oil, in this case, required the combination of the U.S. State Department, the Pentagon, Exxon-Mobil and Unocal Oil company working closely together and developing a close relationship with the Taliban in the process.   The intention, apparently, is for Caspian oil to be piped through a stabilized Afghanistan.

The corporate players consist of Chevron (now Chevron-Texaco), which has been operating in the Tengiz oil field in Kazakhstan since

---

[46]Ayres, Ed. "The Expanding Shadow Economy." World Watch. July/Aug 1996: 21.

1992, Exxon-Mobil, which has been engaged in procuring contracts in Turkmenistan, and the players in the so called $8 billion "contract of the century" in Azerbaijan: BP-Amoco, Unocal, SOCAR (the Azeri state oil company) and Lukoil of Russia. The big question is how to get the oil piped out of the area; what route, through what countries? The oil companies are lobbying up a storm with cash and campaign funds in an effort to get favorable consideration in determining the pipeline routes. Connections with influential Washington insiders does not hurt, people such as Brent Scowcroft and John Sununu who are involved in Azerbaijan, VP Dick Cheney, former CEO of Halliburton, world's largest supplier of oil field peripherals or James Baker, former George Bush senior staffer. The oil companies generally prefer a route through Iran because it is shorter and less expensive to build, except Chevron-Texaco since they are more aligned with the Russians and would prefer a route through Russia using existing pipelines. The Bush administration probably prefers a route through Turkey; even though it would cost billions more, it avoids Iran.[47]

The Baku pipeline from Azerbaijan is a $3.5 billion Exxon project that enjoys a considerable amount of money in the form of loans through the World Bank. The U.S government currently works closely with the dictator of Azerbaijan, Ilham Aliyev, to coordinate the placement of U.S. military troops in the region.[48]

Uzbekistan

Human Rights Watch and Amnesty International have both document-ed in some detail the human rights abuses of Islam Karimov, the dicta-tor in control of Uzbekistan.[49] In December, 2003 Secretary of Defense Donald Rumsfeld was scheduled to meet personally with Karimov. Rumsfeld eventually sent a replacement, but the meeting did take place, in fact Karimov has been a guest at the White House under the Bush Administration. The essential question: were they discussing human rights or were they discussing the acquisition of oil?

---

[47]Chatterjee, Pratap. "Scramble for the Caspian: Big Oil Looks to Divvy Up Caspian Sea Oil Riches." *Multinational Monitor.* Sep 1998: 16-20.

[48]Bookman, Jay. "World Knows Our Foreign Policy Better Than We Do." Atlanta Journal-Constitution. 18 Dec 2003.

[49]Human Rights Watch. World Report 2002. Uzbekistan. www.hrw.org/wr2k2/europe22.html. Amnesty International Report 2002. Uzbekistan. http://web.amnesty.org/web/ar2002.nsf/eur/uzbekistan?Open. *The Independent,* UK, 31 Mar 2004.

Indonesia

According to a lawsuit filed on behalf of 11 indigenous Aceh people by the International Labor Rights Fund, military troops hired by Exxon-Mobil to provide security for their natural gas facility have committed numerous human rights offenses including kidnapping and torture in buildings on the Exxon-Mobil property. Six hundred seventy killings and 161 disappearances have been reported in Aceh; civic leaders and humanitarian workers have been executed since January, 2000. The U.S. Congress had placed a ban on assistance to the Indonesian military because of their involvement in the atrocities in East Timor, but the Bush administration has recently restored military aid to Indonesia.[50]

Sudan

Effects of the acquisition of oil by multi-national oil companies has been reported by Amnesty International and The Society for Threatened Peoples. As a result of two things, the use of local militias to protect the assets of the oil companies and fighting between local groups trying to gain control of oil fields in southern Sudan, there have been an estimated 2 million people killed, 4.5 million displaced and 1 million exiled. Oil field communities have been terrorized and people have been tortured and routed by the oil company militias and government armies in support of the oil companies.[51]

Nigeria

In September, 1998 Amy Goodman of Pacifica Radio reported on the shooting deaths of two Nigerian protesters, Jola Ogungbeje and Aroleka Irowaninu, by the Nigerian Navy and Mobile Police (MOPOL). Surviving protesters claim that the two were shot outright as soon as the military arrived at the protest site in helicopters...helicopters owned and flown by Chevron Oil Corporation. Several other protesters were wounded and eleven others were detained for three weeks. The government owns 60% of the oil operation, while Chevron (now Chevron-Texaco) owns 40%. Interestingly, Nigeria imports 95% of their refined oil products.[52]

One hundred fifty Nigerian women protested the activities of Chevron-Texaco at five pipeline pumping station locations in July, 2002. The

[50]"Exxon-Mobil Sued for Atrocities." *Earth Island Journal.* Winter 2001-2002: 14. See laborrights.org,

[51]"Oil Wells Cause War." Earth Island Journal. Winter 2000-2001: 20.

[52]"Behind the Lines: Chevron Condemned." *Multinational Monitor.* Sept 1998: 4.

[53]Runyon, Curtis. "Nigerian Women Pressure Oil Companies to Promote Change." *World Watch.* Nov/Dec 2002: 6.

protests/occupation shut 1,000 workers out and effectively brought officials of Chevron-Texaco to the bargaining table, if only for a small concession of a $160,000 credit scheme for women to start businesses. Nigeria earns $20 billion annually in oil revenue. The protesters, led by Josephine Ogoba, claim that Chevron-Texaco oil operations across the Niger Delta have caused the destruction of rivers and creeks with toxic pollution, destroyed forests and mangroves, caused noise pollution and air pollution with wellhead gas flaring.[53]

14. Pipelines

There are three problems associated with oil pipelines: (1) sources of funding (2) human rights abuses associated with the building of the pipeline and (3) security/sabotage issues.

They are often funded with money from OPIC, the Export-Import Bank, the International Monetary Fund and the World Bank, that is to say the U.S. taxpayer. Some of the world's wealthiest corporations are recipients of massive welfare; in the words of British Petroleum's CEO John Browne "free public money," or in the words of Representative Ron Paul, Texas Republican, "The majority of Ex-Im Bank funding benefits large, politically powerful corporations."[54]

When the pipeline is built, it is often disruptive to the people and the land through which it is constructed. Large multi-national oil corporations have a record of not being particularly mindful of the harm to the environment and to the indigenous cultures affected.

Pipelines are vulnerable to terrorism and sabotage. There is often a good reason for the desire of locals to destroy a pipeline, although in October 2001 a drunk in Alaska shot the trans-Alaska pipeline with a deer rifle, spilling 300,000 gallons and putting it out of commission for three days.

The 300 mile long Caño Limon pipeline in Colombia has been attacked over one thousand times, 177 alone in 2001. Currently there are 9300 miles of pipeline being constructed in areas of the world that are prone to attacks by local peoples who oppose the pipelines.[55] In the U.S., there are 1.2 million miles of exposed natural gas pipelines with vulnerable central points which control the flow in much of the system. Two

---

[54]Eviatar, Daphne. "Outfront Reports: Public Money in the Pipeline." *Mother Jones.* Jan/Feb 2003: 15.
[55] "Matters of Scale: Trouble in the Pipeline." *World Watch.* May/June 2003: 32.

people in one evening at a few locations in Louisiana could shut down the natural gas supply to a large portion of the east coast. The crude oil pipeline system in Saudi Arabia is also vulnerable to sabotage, and this is not a region where the native population objects. Terrorists who wanted to cut off oil supplies to the U.S. could attack these pipelines with relative ease.

15. Shipping...Oil-Tanker Wrecks, Spills & Air Pollution

Bunker oil is the dirtiest and least expensive liquid fuel available today. It's used by all large ocean going vessels, including oil tankers, of which there are now 92,000 such vessels on the world's oceans carrying 95% of all foreign trade goods. Large vessel traffic is expected to triple in the next 20 years, largely as a result of the World Trade Organization (WTO) agreements. Large ocean going vessels are the only completely unregulated transportation source of pollution, and yet are one of the biggest pollution sources. According to a recent report from Bluewater Network, *A Stacked Deck: Air Pollution From Ships*, because of the failure of the EPA or any other international agency to regulate these emissions, shipping has become a major factor in global warming pollution, acid rain and smog...even smog at sea.[56] New studies by Carnegie Mellon University show that 14% of global nitrogen oxide emissions and 16% of all sulfur dioxide emissions from all petroleum sources come from ships at sea.[57] The reason bunker oil is the world's dirtiest fuel is because it is unrefined, containing high amounts of toxic compounds that are banned from use in all other applications. Bunker oil has 1000 times more sulfur, for example, than diesel fuel used in buses and trucks on the road.

The possibility of remedy is not hopeful because of the power of U.S. and European ship owners, although an organ of the U.N. (the International Maritime Organization) in 1997 tried to add an annex to the International Convention on the Prevention of Pollution from Ships (MARPOL, Annex VI), but to no avail. Additional effort has come from the organization Bluewater which filed a lawsuit in February, 2000 to get the EPA to set emission standards for ocean going ships.

Tanker spills

The Prestige, which sank off the Spanish coast in November, 2002, was a single hulled oil tanker carrying 24 million gallons of highly toxic

---

[56]Long, Russell. "Stacked Decks: Trading Air Quality for Global Trade." *Earth Island Journal.* Winter 2000-2001: 8.

[57]"Dirtying the Trade Winds." *Earth Island Journal.* Winter 1999-2000: 19.

cargo -- twice as much as the *Exxon Valdez* which created an ecological disaster off the coast of Alaska in 1989. *The Prestige* has been described by authorities as an "aging rust bucket" that should have been retired to the dustbin years ago. This could be one of the worst shipping related oil spills ever, and yet the political will to do anything about it is questionable, given the political clout of the industry and the complexity of the problem. *The Prestige* itself was registered in a tax haven, the Bahamas, built by the Japanese, owned by a company registered in Liberia, managed by a Greek firm, certified by an American organization, chartered by a Swiss based Russian trading company, and carrying oil from Latvia to Singapore. Four such single hulled tankers have sunk in recent years and the requirement for double hulls won't take effect until 2015. No one knows why *The Prestige* broke up in heavy seas. The American Bureau of Shipping (ABS) claims that they inspected it in May, 2001, and it was in conformity with their requirements. It has been suggested by David Fantillo, a scientist with Greenpeace in England, that the inspection procedure may be flawed or was not done properly. Assessing liability will be next to impossible because of the web of responsibilities; the fishing industry in Spain will not be helped even if blame can be fixed. Even with changes, double hulls are also not immune to disaster as the sinking of the *Levoli Sun* off the coast of Normandy in 2000 attests.

16. Terrorism, Embargoes, Price Instability

Terrorism is a persistent problem regarding pipelines because often oil companies destroy and pollute indigenous homelands in the process of building pipelines.

The OPEC oil embargo of 1973 illustrated that when supplies are withheld from the U.S., the result is chaos. In this case, when the oil spigot was turned back on, it cost the U.S. importers four times as much per barrel as before the boycott by OPEC. Throughout the 1970s, the OPEC nations kept the oil supply constrained keeping prices high...and there was nothing we could do about it. The U.S. now has a negative trade balance of over $150 billion per year to purchase foreign oil.

According to Prince Bandar al Sultan, the Saudi minister to the U.S., Saudi Arabia and OPEC do not want the price of oil to go too much above $28 per barrel, and they would prefer a price of about $25.[58] Prince Bandar claims that it is good for the U.S. if the price stays below

---

[58]Russert, Tim. Interview. Meet The Press. with Prince Bandar al Sultan. NBC. 25 April 2004.

$28. What Prince Bandar didn't say is that above $28, it becomes economically feasible to replace Saudi oil with synthetic fuels by using such processes as Fischer-Tropsch chemistry or the Mobil-M process for the conversion of coal gases or methanol into gasoline (page 56-60).

17. Cleaning Up The Mess
Flaring at the wellhead

Flaring is the burning off of associated natural gas that is dissolved in the oil being extracted from the ground. The gas is separated from the oil at the wellhead and burned in a continuous flame sometimes reaching one hundred feet into the air. Along with the flame, of course, is the attendant unburned methane, sulfur compounds and carbon dioxide. Per ton, methane has twenty times more global warming impact than carbon dioxide.

Chevron-Texaco has been operating in the Niger delta for forty years and is currently flaring over 5 million cubic feet of natural gas per day, which accounts for 20% of all flared gas in the world. The technologies exist to safely re-inject the gas into the ground, but companies, such as Chevron-Texaco and Shell, choose instead to pay a fine of 11 cents per 1000 cubic feet of flared gas and continue to flare, even though it causes such harm. Likewise, the oil corporations have determined that it is not profitable enough to recover the gas and sell it because there is not a large enough market in places such as Nigeria. Flaring of associated natural gas in Nigeria alone puts 35 million tons of carbon dioxide into the atmosphere every year.[59]

Banned in the U.S. for good reason, flaring continues in areas around the world where national governments have no power to stop it, or, if they have been co-opted by the oil corporations, no desire to stop it. Local indigenous peoples are now demanding that the flaring be stopped, and they be compensated for the many years of injury to their health, environment and economy.

JP-8 health effects

Since introduced onto air bases in the 1990s as a replacement for JP-4, JP-8 jet fuel has come under increasing scrutiny as a cancer-causing agent and as a severe immune system depressant. It consists of a mixture of hydrocarbons, some of which are known carcinogens such as benzene, naphthalene and polyaromatic hydrocarbons (PAHs) that

---

[59]Burning & Looting: Flaring in the Delta. Project Underground: Nigeria. www.moles.org/ProjectUnderground/oil/nigeria/burning.html.

according to studies, are inhaled by virtually everyone near an active air base. Tests on animals in Britain have shown that it can cause lung, kidney and liver damage as well as extreme toxicity to the immune system. Mark Witten, a toxicologist at the University of Arizona, studied its effects with Air Force funding and found that when mice inhale it, their immune system is wrecked; "I've never seen a chemical that can so completely wipe out an animal's defenses" says Witten. Witten found that after only brief exposure the thymus (where immune cells mature) shrinks and the immune "T" cells plummet, while "B" cells proliferate. A possible mechanism is that the fuel doesn't readily evaporate, so it's more likely to soak into the lungs and skin. Furthermore, the chemical additives to the fuel also cause it to disrupt the molecules of the outermost layer of skin on humans breaking the natural barrier to alien chemicals.

The effects are so severe and sustained that the researchers are warning that repeated exposure to JP-8 could increase the risk of autoimmune diseases and cancer. Senator Reid of Nevada has asked for a study at Fallon Air base in Nevada where a cluster of 14 childhood leukemia cases point to JP-8 as a causative agent. Thirteen of the fourteen confirmed cases are acute lymphoblastic leukemia, and it is already known that children of parents who are exposed to hydrocarbons at work have a greater risk of developing this type of cancer. When pregnant mice are exposed, up to 70% of their offspring die and the ones that do survive have abnormal white blood cells. No studies have yet been done on the effects of exposure to children and pregnant women. Leukemia expert Peter Domer at the University of Chicago agrees that Witten's concerns are well founded; the U.S. Navy denies that JP-8 poses a risk. The Pentagon wants to use JP-8 as a "universal" fuel to power jet aircraft as well as trucks, stoves, tanks, etc. because of its many military advantages.[60]

18. Subsidies and Giveaways

The idea of government subsidies is that they are supposed to be a way to allow promising new and emerging technologies to get from the concept phase of development to a commercial production phase. Without the financial help to get started, good ideas would be lost and the benefits of large scale commercialization would never be realized. When established corporations operating in mature industries find them-

---

[60]"In The Firing Line." *New Scientist.* June 18, 2001: 7.

selves on the receiving end of huge government handouts, it falls under the category of corporate welfare and in fact destroys the opportunities for deserving emerging technologies to develop. The rich get richer, and the breakthrough technologies end up in countries that have more progressive and less politically dependent funding mechanisms.

Subsidies and giveaways to the oil and gas industries fall into three broad areas: (1) direct handouts from the treasury of the U.S. (2) the use of the military to acquire and protect corporate oil interests overseas and (3) externalities, shifting external expenses from the corporations who are responsible to the public.

In all cases, we should be aware of the benefits that are accrued by private corporate interests at the expense of the public; the phenomenon, as discussed in Chapter Two, of socialized costs but privatized profits.

Handouts from the U.S. Treasury
Pending energy legislation (September 2004) gives about $50 billion in handouts to the oil, gas, coal and nuclear industries, $13 billion alone in tax subsidies.

The question remains; why would a mature industry be subsidized at all, especially in a "free market" society where welfare and handouts are officially scorned?

Use of the Military
In Colombia, the U.S. pays several billion dollars as part of "Plan Colombia," of which over $100 million per year is designated specifically for training Colombian troops to protect the Occidental Petroleum pipeline. This is calculated by AmazonWatch to be a subsidy of between $4 and $24 per barrel (depending on the amount pumped through the pipeline) to Occidental; it is not a direct giveaway to Occidental but the oil company benefits directly.

The current U.S. involvement in Iraq, according to papers released through the Freedom Of Information Act in a lawsuit brought by Sierra Club and Judicial Watch, had everything to do with oil and how it was to be divided up.[61] If the military costs were to be included in the cost

---

[61] Everest, Larry, "Cheney, Energy and Iraq War." *The San Francisco Chronicle.* 21 Mar 2004.. *Cheney Energy Task Force Documents Feature Maps of Iraqi Oilfields.* Judicial Watch. www.judicialwatch.org/071703.b_PR.shtml.

of the Iraqi oil, it would bring the price up from $40 per barrel to $235 per barrel. This does not include, of course, the misery and loss of life associated with this adventure.

Externalities
Subsidy assessments to the oil and gas industries in the U.S. will vary widely depending upon measurement approaches; the primary variable factor being the impact upon surrounding populations of externalities for which the people are not compensated.

For example, in the Oriente region of Ecuador, Texaco knowingly dumped 4.3 million gallons of toxic waste per day onto the ground near their operations. This amounted to a $3 per barrel subsidy to Texaco in avoided costs for the responsible disposal of the waste.

Most people acknowledge that the oil industry is heavily subsidized, generally conceding about $2 per gallon of gasoline equivalent, but according to a 1999 study from the International Center for Technology Assessment, the figure should be in the range of $15 not $2. They figure in the billions per year in federal and state tax breaks, federal subsidies, regulation, pollution cleanup and other factors. Externalities attributed to the oil industry total a minimum of $558 billion per year, and a case is made for subsidies totaling upwards of $1.69 trillion per year.[62]

---

[62]Ayres, Ed. "Out of Touch." *World Watch*. Sept/Oct 2002: 4.

4 How Much Energy Do We Need?

HOW MUCH END USE ENERGY DO WE NEED?

When considering society's energy needs, the real questions we need to ask are: 'what do we need to do,' and 'what services do we want' and 'how much energy do these things require.' We want a cold drink, a hot shower, and to be able to get from one place to another in comfort. We don't need the energy itself, we need the service that the energy provides. A cold drink is a cold drink; a slightly warmer drink is not acceptable even if it may save some energy. The condition then is that no one does with less, no one is asked to sacrifice comfort and no one is asked to pay more for the goods or services that the end use energy provides.

We know that we need end use energy in three forms: liquid fuel, heat and electricity. Liquid fuel is used primarily for transportation, heat for a combination of space heat and domestic hot water, and electricity for a wide variety of uses such as lights, motors, electronics and appliances. The question remains: how much energy do we need?

Transportation
The personal transportation demand for the U.S. is 3 trillion miles per year...in comfort, and being able to haul what needs to be hauled.

The fleet for the U.S. is about 130 million cars and light trucks, with about 16 million or so new vehicles being sold each year. We will assume that it is possible to make large plug in diesel hybrid electric vehicles (PDHEVs), which obtain the equivalent of 300 mpg of liquid fuel, available to the new car market at a rate of ten million per year, eventually replacing the current fleet, which now averages less than 25 mpg. The new fleet of PDHEVs would include the styles and models

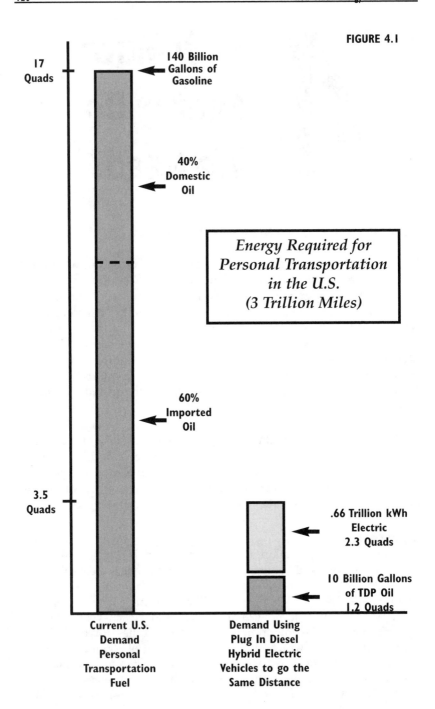

FIGURE 4.1

17 Quads

140 Billion Gallons of Gasoline

40% Domestic Oil

Energy Required for Personal Transportation in the U.S. (3 Trillion Miles)

60% Imported Oil

3.5 Quads

.66 Trillion kWh Electric 2.3 Quads

10 Billion Gallons of TDP Oil 1.2 Quads

Current U.S. Demand Personal Transportation Fuel

Demand Using Plug In Diesel Hybrid Electric Vehicles to go the Same Distance that the consumer wants including full sized SUVs and small trucks. In 2003, the U.S. consumed 140 billion gallons of gasoline to go that distance. Chapter Six will show how the 3 trillion miles can be covered using 10 billion gallons of liquid fuel, a reduction of over 90% (Figure 4.1).

Of the 3 trillion miles traveled, about 80% of the miles are trips of fewer than 60 miles (2.4 trillion miles), and the rest are highway miles at cruising speed. The secret is to have two motors and use liquid fuel only where necessary (cruising on the highway), and use electricity where possible because electricity can be derived from renewable primary energy.

With a new generation of batteries, including lithium-polymer, lithium-sulfur and alkaline zinc/matrix technologies, a PDHEV can go the 60 miles on battery power without having to carry around 900 pounds of batteries. The battery pack weighs less than 100 pounds and is recharged while under way with regenerative braking and by starting up the small diesel engine. If there is a need to pass or accelerate while on the highway, a flip of the switch will kick in 180 HP of electric motors for instant acceleration, the batteries having been fully charged with the diesel engine while underway.

Space heat and domestic hot water
The U.S. demand for residential and commercial space heat and hot water is about 8 quads (8 quads = 8 X 10^{15} BTU) of energy, mostly in the form of natural gas as the primary energy source.

Residential and commercial requirements are considered here, omitting for simplicity sake the demand for industrial space and process heat. About 40% of the 8 quads of primary energy could be avoided with some reasonable efficiency measures being incorporated at the same time that passive solar or solar thermal systems are put into place. ZEH (Zero Energy Homes) projects in the U.S. have shown that with very good design, homes can be operated with no outside energy requirement. Studies in Canada have shown that with minor modifications in design, proper insulation and reasonable conservation measures, heating demand can be cut in half. In other words the 8 quads demand could quickly drop to 4 quads, but we will use 8 quads in our graphics to be conservative.

This book introduces a new source of free heat: heat recovered from the high temperature fuel cell, whose primary function is to generate electricity, but which allows for up to 40% of the input energy to be recovered for space heating and domestic hot water at water temperatures of up to 1000°F.

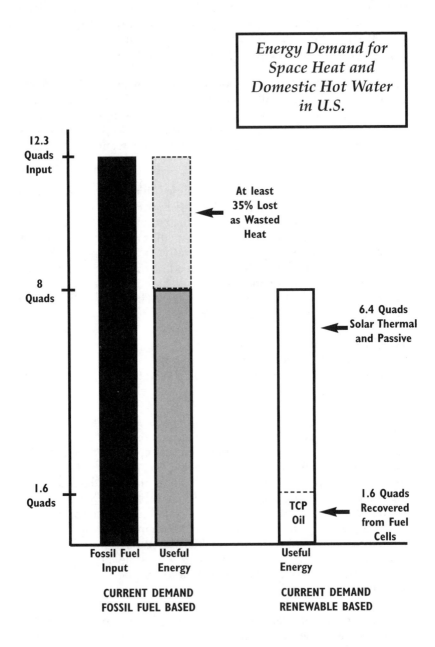

FIGURE 4.2

Electricity

The amount of U.S. electrical use is somewhat over 3 trillion kWh per year -- electrical energy measured at the meters of all residential, commercial and industrial customers. We will use the figure 3.145 trillion kWh per year.

The total amount of electricity generated is somewhat more than that because of losses in transmission and distribution (10%) and electrical losses within the generating plant (5%).

In a fuel cell, a photovoltaic array or a wind generator, the electricity is generated as direct current (DC). If the power is generated on site (distributed generation, DG) it becomes feasible to use the DC directly instead of converting it into alternating current (AC). DC is more efficient in motors, for lighting, for electronics and computers and many appliances. Theoretically, the energy savings for using DC directly and not converting to AC could approach 50%, we will assume a gain of 25% here.[1] This would bring the total demand to 2.35 trillion kWh. Added to the electrical demand is .65 trillion kWh for charging the PDHEVs for a new total demand of 3 trillion kWh per year. About what it was before, but now including enough electrical energy to carry a PDHEV 2.4 trillion miles.

An Example of More Efficient Use of Electrical Energy

The energy supplied to computers is 60 cycle/120 volt AC (alternating current)power, but the computer converts the AC power to 12V, 5V and 3.3V DC (direct current) internally. There is a loss of up to 40% associated with this conversion. If DC was supplied, as it could be using photovoltaics (PV), distributed generation wind or fuel cells, all of which generate DC current, the loss could be lessened to 10%.

With 205 million PCs in the U.S., which average 300 kWh per year consumption, by increasing the efficiency 60% to 90%, it would save 20.5 billion kWh or $1.64 billion per year at 8 cents per kWh. Motors and many other electrical devices run more efficiently on DC than they do on AC.

The U.S. economy needs about 20 quads of end use energy per year. With the new way, we will get the beneficial use of 20 quads of energy,

---

1 A 10% gain is achieved immediately by not using an inverter to convert the DC to AC. The larger gains come from the inherent efficiencies of DC motors and lighting.

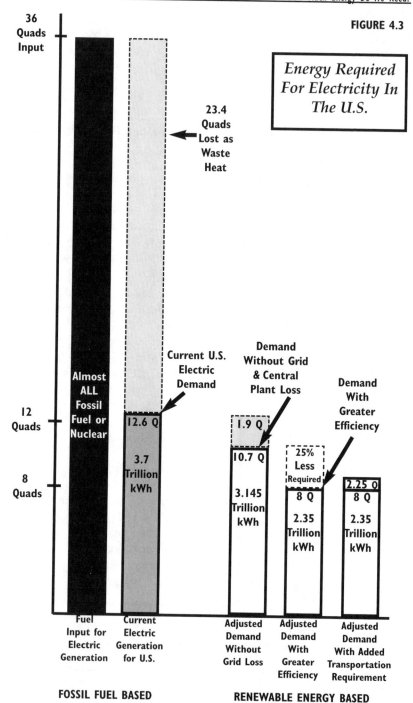

FIGURE 4.3

Energy Required For Electricity In The U.S.

36 Quads Input

23.4 Quads Lost as Waste Heat

12 Quads

8 Quads

Almost ALL Fossil Fuel or Nuclear

Current U.S. Electric Demand

12.6 Q

3.7 Trillion kWh

Demand Without Grid & Central Plant Loss

1.9 Q

10.7 Q

3.145 Trillion kWh

Demand With Greater Efficiency

25% Less Required

8 Q

2.35 Trillion kWh

2.25 Q

8 Q

2.35 Trillion kWh

Fuel Input for Electric Generation

Current Electric Generation for U.S.

Adjusted Demand Without Grid Loss

Adjusted Demand With Greater Efficiency

Adjusted Demand With Added Transportation Requirement

FOSSIL FUEL BASED   **RENEWABLE ENERGY BASED**

FIGURE 4.4

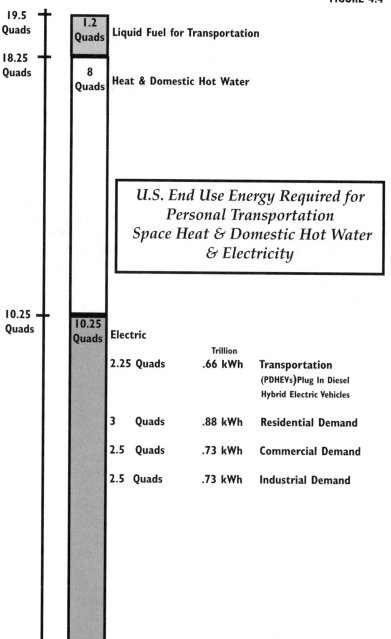

19.5 Quads

1.2 Quads — Liquid Fuel for Transportation

18.25 Quads

8 Quads — Heat & Domestic Hot Water

U.S. End Use Energy Required for Personal Transportation Space Heat & Domestic Hot Water & Electricity

10.25 Quads

10.25 Quads — Electric

	Trillion	
2.25 Quads	.66 kWh	**Transportation** (PDHEVs)Plug In Diesel Hybrid Electric Vehicles
3 Quads	.88 kWh	**Residential Demand**
2.5 Quads	.73 kWh	**Commercial Demand**
2.5 Quads	.73 kWh	**Industrial Demand**

but when we compare inputs into the two systems -- the old (fossil fuel/nuclear) and the new (renewable energy) -- we see that the input into our economy now is on the order of 100 quads of energy (all primary energy coming into the system). The input into the entire system under the new scenario is reduced to 12.4 quads. By transitioning from the old way (100 quads input) to the new way (12.4 quads input), we achieve a savings of 87.6 quads. It is possible to use just a little over 12% of the energy we used in the past to achieve the same, or better, results.

Technically, and especially politically, it is probably not possible to achieve this theoretical 88% energy savings. The illustration does show convincingly that (a) a tremendous amount of primary energy is currently wasted and (b) dramatic improvements to the way we convert primary energy to useful energy are possible. In order to better understand why policy decisions and funding priorities do not favor increasing efficiency and the development of improved technologies, Chapter Seven looks at who might benefit from resisting such change, and what political power they have.

5 How Much Energy Do We Have?

AVAILABLE RENEWABLE PRIMARY ENERGY

Whenever the topic of renewable energy is discussed in the media, inevitably someone brings up the point that despite its many advantages, we simply do not have enough of it. This myth should be cast into the bin of urban legends. In reality, we have about five times more primary energy, in renewable form, than we need...an endless supply. The primary energy is found in five main areas: waste, biomass, wind, sun and ocean systems. There is also a fifth category, "other," that includes a wide range of exciting new sources of clean primary energy.

Currently, the total primary energy entering the U.S. system is about 100 quads, with about 36 quads of that available to the consumer as end use energy. With reasonable demand-side efficiency measures, the 36 quads of demand can be reduced to around 20 quads. The difference of 16 quads, however, is not central to our discussion because There are 100 to 120 quads of clean renewable primary energy available. Whether there are three times more (100/36) or six times more (120/20) than is needed is academic.

It is also important to note here that when replacing the old way with a new way, it is not necessary to replace the 100 quads of primary energy required by the old way. Demand must be accommodated, which is 36 quads or with efficiency measures in place 20 quads. It is also important to note that there is no need for foreign oil, there is no need for nuclear energy, and there is no need for coal fired plants, nor is there even a need for an electrical grid. Furthermore, the new way of acquiring energy would produce millions of good jobs, would greatly reduce our $570 billion trade imbalance, would enhance national security and would leave a legacy to future generations of which we are not ashamed. Two important concepts, coupled with the idea of an all-renewable primary energy economy, are conservation/efficiency and distributed generation as discussed in Chapter Two.

WASTE AND BIOMASS
A billion tons of free energy

Figure 5.1 shows how 12 quads of equivalent thermal energy can be derived from waste streams and biomass conversion. This number assumes a conversion efficiency of less than 70% from feedstock to fuel oil using thermal conversion (TCP) type processes. Not counted are useful and valuable by-products from the TC process other than fuel oil, such as activated carbon, syn-gas, metals, hydrochloric acid and fertilizer grade chemicals. Please note that energy content of feedstock material varies widely and conversion efficiencies to a fuel oil product also vary. Also note that there are technologies other than TCP that can economically convert waste and biomass into liquid fuels.

The economics of the various types of "gas to liquid" processes such as methanol synthesis or methanol to high volumetric energy content liquid fuels are highly dependent on the market price of crude oil. The rule of thumb break point is about $25 to $28 per barrel of oil. This means that whenever the price of crude exceeds $25 per barrel[1] or so, then these alternative processes become profitable. This is also the real reason that OPEC publically announces that they want the price of oil to be below $28 per barrel. Note that the cost to manufacture TCP oil is under $12 per barrel and is expected to go below $8 per barrel when greater numbers of plants go online. Other gas to liquid processes produce synthetic fuels in the $25-$28 per barrel range.

When comparing total BTU input of feedstock to the thermal energy content of the 100 billion gallons of TCP oil, shown in Figure 5.1, the plant efficiency would only have to be about 36%. When using high grade feedstock such as used tires or plastic, the TCP efficiencies actually range to above 90% and average above 80%. The chart shows an average energy content of all feedstock at 18 million BTUs per ton. See Chapter One for the discussion of liquid fuel production other than TCP oil such as methanol synthesis, cellulosic ethanol, Fisher-Tropsch fuels, Mobil-M fuels, fast pyrolysis "bio-oil," hydrocarbon synthesis, etc. It would be expected that the plant efficiencies for any of these processes would exceed 36%.

---

[1] See Chapter Six for the real price of oil, which when externalities are added comes to more like $235-$400 per barrel not the $40 market price reported

ANNUAL WASTE AND BIOMASS RESOURCES FOR THE U.S.
100 billion gallons of light fuel oil per year can be produced from waste and biomass.

Source of Waste Energy Content	Millions of Tons Per Year	TCP fuel oil (Gallons per Ton)	Potential Oil Production (Billions of Gallons)
Municipal Solid Waste 7,500 BTU/lb	200	70	14
Municipal Sewage Sludge, Hazmat 2,400 BTU/lb @20% solids	5.6 dry sludge 9.4 Hazmat	100	1.5
Agricultural Crop Waste, recoverable 7,300 BTU/lb	350 dry	35	13
Feedlot manure 1200 BTU/lb @10% solids	220 total collectable	100	22
Plastics 18,000 BTU/lb	20	260	5.2
Tires 15,000 BTU/lb	4	130	0.5
Heavy Oil or Tar Sands 21,000 BTU/lb	50 @5% of crude	215	10.7
Forestry Waste 8,000 BTU/lb	40-200	35	7
Restaurant Grease SVO 60,000 BTU/lb. equivalent energy	3	300 equiv. energy	1
Energy Crops Grown on Idle Land 3-8 Tons/acre 7,300 BTU/lb Switchgrass	50 million acres 150-400	35	11 @ 6.5 tons/acre
Energy Crops grown on 15% of cropland 3-8 tons/acre, 7,300 BTU/lb Switchgrass	100 million acres 300-800	35	22 @ 6.5 tons/acre
Totals	Up to 2 billion tons of waste and biomass		100 billion gallons of fuel oil

Figure 5.1

TCP is an emerging technology that is just now being implemented on a commercial scale. Chapter One also examined several other technologies related to thermal depolymerization in varying degrees of development, such as fast pyrolysis. Feedstocks can include just about anything that is non-radioactive, hence, the wide variety of material included on the waste and biomass resources chart and the large number for tonnage of potential feedstock material, which is well over a billion tons per year for the U.S.

Figure 5.1 shows about one billion tons of collectable waste and one billion tons of biomass that could be grown without adversely affecting food prices or soil fertility. The waste streams listed in Figure 5.1 can also be converted to methanol, which can be used to fire fuel cells directly or converted to higher energy content liquid fuels such as gasoline or dimethyl ether (DME).

WIND
The energy in moving air

The energy resources contained in winds in the U.S. are well known and mapped in detail. Since the performance of modern wind generators is also well documented, it is not difficult to calculate the amount of energy that could be practically extracted from this resource.

Wind Energy as Exponential Function

The energy in wind is a cubed function of wind speed, which means that if the wind speed doubles there is eight times as much available energy, not twice as much as one might expect. This concept illustrates the importance of the Stanford study when one considers that in order to achieve the 24% increase in overall energy the wind speed would only have to be increased by 7.5% from 16 mph to 17.2 mph.

This increase in available energy is figured according to the formula $(1+r)^n$ where 'r' is the percentage change and 'n' is the number of times it is multiplied by itself. In this example; $(1.075)^3$ = 1.24   A 7.5% increase in wind speed produces a 24% increase in energy, which illustrates the cubed function of energy and wind speed.

There are many factors to be taken into account, such as the land area required, access to the generators, aesthetics and other disruptions. However, the fact remains that the energy content in moving air is massive and, therefore, valuable, plus it's free, it's clean, and most importantly, it can be accessed by local communities and individuals. The "power shift" in this case has great implications for those interested in, and for those who are in a position to convert moving air into electrical energy.

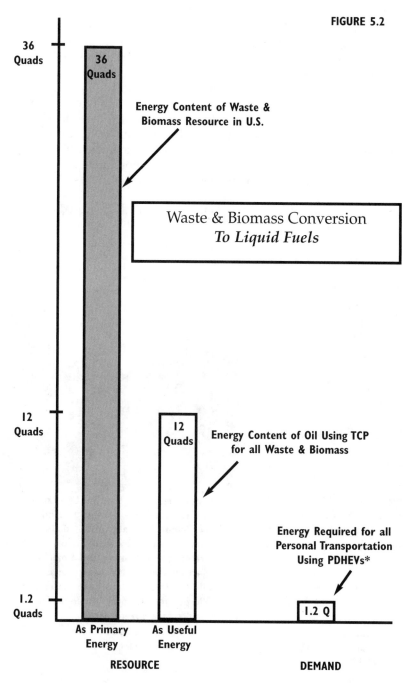

FIGURE 5.2

36 Quads

36 Quads

Energy Content of Waste & Biomass Resource in U.S.

Waste & Biomass Conversion
To Liquid Fuels

12 Quads

12 Quads

Energy Content of Oil Using TCP for all Waste & Biomass

Energy Required for all Personal Transportation Using PDHEVs*

1.2 Quads

1.2 Q

As Primary Energy   As Useful Energy

RESOURCE   DEMAND

*Plug in Diesel Hybrid Electric Vehicle liquid fuel demand.

Wind resources are measured in kilowatt-hours (kWh) per year of potential electricity that could be extracted from a particular area, usually a state. The resource numbers are based on many years of surveys of average wind speed at a certain height, typically 164 feet (50 meters) above ground level. The numbers reflect the practical amount of energy that can be extracted, not the greatest theoretical amount. The numbers are conservative for another reason. A new study conducted by Stanford University found that if the wind speed averages are calculated at 230 feet (70 meters) instead of 164 feet above the ground, the amount of available energy is actually 24% greater than the resource data now shows. The 230-foot level reflects more accurately the hub height of the larger, newer wind generators now being installed.

The ten states with the best wind energy potential, measured in trillion kWh per year are:

1. Kansas   1.6
2. Texas   1.6
3. North Dakota 1.5
4. Nebraska   1.3
5. South Dakota 1.2
6. Oklahoma   1
7. Montana   1
8. Minnesota   1
9. Wyoming   0.9
10. Iowa   0.9

When we compare the ten state total of 12 trillion kWh per year to the total demand for the U.S. of about 3 trillion kWh per year,[2] we can readily see the quantity of excess renewable primary energy (Figure 5.3).

Photo, near Mendota Hills in Lee County, IL, shows an access road -- through a cornfield -- to an 800 KW wind generator installed about a half mile from the county road. The access road and wind site took less than one and a half acres out of production. This 50 MW wind project will add $50 million to the local tax base, provide $130,000 per year to local farmers as lease payments and create dozens of jobs.

[2]Wind data as published in the US PIRG Education Fund Report 2003 which can be read in full at www.pirg.org PIRG credits the Union of Concerned Scientists for the data which includes areas of class 3 and greater, land areas only within 20 miles of existing transmission lines, excluding all urban area, excluding all environmentally sensitive area, 50% of forested areas, excluding 30% of agricultural land and excluding 10% of all range land.

FIGURE 5.3

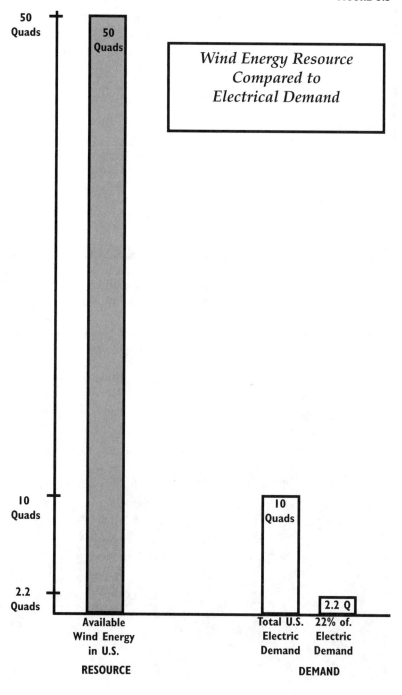

Wind Energy Resource
Compared to
Electrical Demand

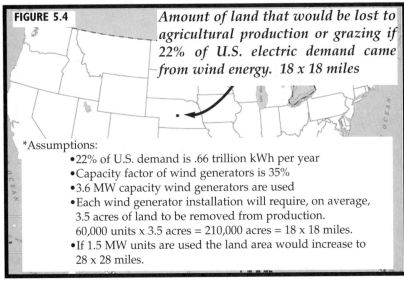

FIGURE 5.4

Amount of land that would be lost to agricultural production or grazing if 22% of U.S. electric demand came from wind energy. 18 x 18 miles

*Assumptions:
- 22% of U.S. demand is .66 trillion kWh per year
- Capacity factor of wind generators is 35%
- 3.6 MW capacity wind generators are used
- Each wind generator installation will require, on average, 3.5 acres of land to be removed from production.
  60,000 units x 3.5 acres = 210,000 acres = 18 x 18 miles.
- If 1.5 MW units are used the land area would increase to 28 x 28 miles.

FIGURE 5.4 (above) illustrates the enormous amount of energy contained in moving air. The little square shows the land area 18 miles x 18 miles that would be required to furnish 22% of the U.S. electrical demand with wind energy.

Photo (below) shows a substation near a small wind project near Garrett, Pennsylvania. The land requirement for the substation is approximately 3 acres.

THE SUN
Free photons, free heat
Radiant energy, in the form of photons, strikes the surface of the earth with the average equivalent of about 167 kWh of energy (equal to 570,000 BTUs thermal energy) per square foot per year. It varies with locale, cloud cover and orientation of the surface, but 167 kWh is a fair approximation for the U.S. The question then becomes, how much of this energy can be economically and practically captured and put to use? The average household requires on the order of 8,000-10,000 kWh per year of electricity before efficiency measures are put into place. The country requires about three trillion kWh per year (3×10^{12} kWh) for all demand. The limiting factor becomes available space in which to install the collection devices, not the amount of potential available energy.

Land area required to supply 3 trillion kWh, the total demand for the U.S., is about 100 miles by 100 miles with 73% coverage of PV collectors operating at 10.4% efficiency. It wouldn't be feasible to generate all of the electricity in one remote location of course; after all photovoltaics are the ideal distributed form of generation; they can be placed virtually anywhere.

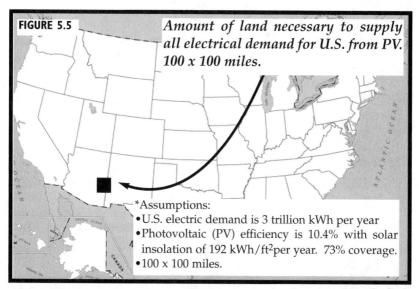

FIGURE 5.5

Amount of land necessary to supply all electrical demand for U.S. from PV. 100 x 100 miles.

*Assumptions:
• U.S. electric demand is 3 trillion kWh per year
• Photovoltaic (PV) efficiency is 10.4% with solar insolation of 192 kWh/ft²per year. 73% coverage.
• 100 x 100 miles.

FIGURE 5.5 (above) shows the land area of 100 miles x 100 miles that would be required to furnish all of the U.S. electrical demand using photovoltaics.

A more practical calculation would be one that had PV supplying 25% of demand and placed on rooftops throughout the country. If 20,000 square feet of PV were installed on 33% of the super sized "box" stores (1.65 million of them) and 400 square feet of PV were installed on 25% of the homes in the U.S. (25 million of them), it would total 43 billion square feet of collection. At a conservative 10.4% efficiency, 750 billion kWh per year would be generated, or 25% of the total demand for the country

OTHER RENEWABLE ENERGY RESOURCES

While some of the more exotic new emerging technologies are exciting, it's difficult to calculate how much effect they will have as primary energy resources. There is enough data to arrive at a fair estimation for offshore wind and geothermal. The potential of ocean systems remains to be seen.

Offshore Wind

The wind resource figures for the U.S. do not include offshore, where there is great wind energy potential, particularly in the population

dense Northeast, and especially off the coast of Long Island, New York where consumers pay up to 16 cents per kWh.

Northeast U.S. offshore wind energy potential is estimated at over 220,000 MW, enough to produce 770 billion kWh of electricity per year or 25% of the entire demand for the U.S. This includes the area between 5 and 50 nautical miles from shore between New York City and Canada. Larger turbines can be used in offshore installations (photo left) where winds are more consistent and of greater velocity.

Photo courtesy of AMEC Project Investments Limited, Northumberland, U.K. AMEC is a joint developer of the U.K.'s first offshore multi-megawatt wind turbines at Blyth.

In the U.S., the population dense East Coast has about 8,500 square miles of excellent potential wind site area where the water depth is less than 70 feet and there are no land use restrictions. This wind energy potential would be the equivalent of about two quads of thermal energy or enough to furnish half the electrical demand for the Northeast U.S.

Geothermal
Energy from the interior of the Earth
Energy is contained as heat in the earth's interior, but it is near enough to the surface to be able to economically extract it.

Fourteen western states have significant geothermal potential, according to a recent Department of Energy/ Department of Interior study. They identified 271 cities, all within five miles of geothermal resources, that could utilize geothermal energy for district heating or electrical generation. It is estimated that the recoverable potential is about two quads of thermal energy.

In order to extract energy from geothermal resources, a well must be drilled several thousand feet into the ground to reach the source of heat, a brine saturated solution of water about 500°F. This hot brine solution is pumped to the surface and heat is extracted from it with a heat exchanger, and the brine is returned to the ground. The exchanged heat drives a turbine which generates electricity.

CONCLUSION

As we see from Figure 5.7,the U.S. has five times as much energy as we need, all from clean, renewable sources. We only need to use what is available to us. The resources exist, for example, in the form of wind, biomass, sun, ocean power and even grease. The choice is to either throw the grease out...or use it as a fuel.

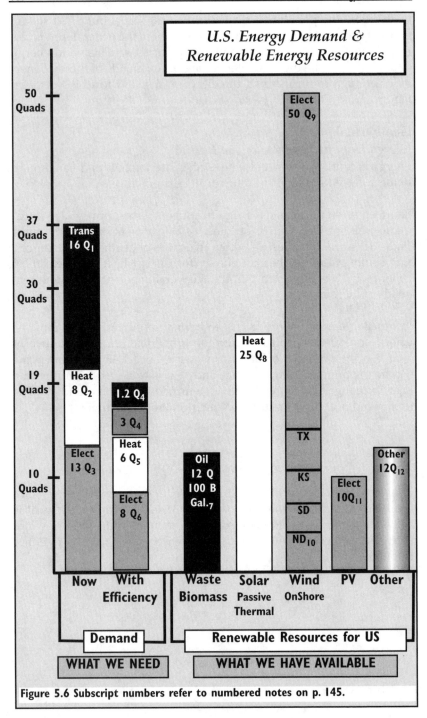

Figure 5.6 Subscript numbers refer to numbered notes on p. 145.

Notes to Figure 5.6

1. 16 quads represents 140 billion gallons of gasoline and diesel fuel, which presently serves the fleet of 130 million cars and light trucks. The total personal transportation mileage driven per year is on the order of 3 trillion miles with a fleet average of about 21 mpg.

2. 8 quads represents the space heat and domestic hot water demand for all current residential and commercial use.

3. 13 quads represents the thermal equivalent of 3.75 trillion kWh of electrical generation. This is the electricity for all residential, commercial and industrial use today.

4. 1.2 quads represents the energy in 10 billion gallons of TCP oil.

5. 6 quads represents the required demand for all space heat and domestic hot water with the implementation of passive solar upgrades to some existing homes and commercial buildings and the installation of thermal solar collectors on most homes in the U.S.

6. 8 quads represents the electrical demand with inherent efficiencies of distributed generation and SOFC (solid oxide fuel cell) use.

7. 12 quads represents the thermal energy contained in the fuel oil that could be derived from waste and biomass resources in the U.S.

8. 25 quads represents the energy available if passive solar retrofits were widely constructed and solar thermal collectors were installed on most homes and commercial buildings.

9. 50 quads represents the thermal equivalent of electricity that could be generated from the land based wind resources in the U.S. This only includes good wind sites and is the practical amount of energy that could be extracted, not the theoretical maximum.

10. A few states are shown as indicated. For example, North Dakota has at least 1.5 trillion kWh (equal to about 5 quads of energy) of extractable wind energy, as electricity, available per year. This one state exceeds the current residential demand of the entire U.S.

11. 10 quad represents the amount of electricity that could be generated if all homes and commercial buildings were equipped with PV modules. For example, every home would have a module of 24'x24' in size, commercial buildings somewhat larger.

12. Other forms of primary energy such as offshore wind, ocean systems, geothermal, etc., would be able to contribute about 12 quads of energy if they were developed.

6 Economic Strategies

The U.S. economy is currently based on fossil fuels and nuclear energy, for which there are certain costs that are not necessary with a renewable energy economy. Some of these cost penalties can be quantified fairly precisely, some cannot...the costs remain. Some are paid for by the consumer, some by the public at large. If we were to attach costs to the items on the list below, they would easily total $750 billion per year,[1] a more realistic number would be in the $900 billion range, and a case could be made for well over a trillion dollars per year, depending on how one accounts for externalities and clean up costs. To be conservative, we will use $750 billion per year. Renewable energy has a $750 billion advantage because with renewable energy:

- The primary energy is free, and it is converted into useful energy more efficiently

- There is no need for foreign oil, reducing the trade deficit

- There is a reduced need for an electrical grid

- Subsidies to the oil, gas, coal and nuclear industries can be eliminated...we no longer need foreign oil or nuclear power

- There are no clean up costs and no externalities

- There is no longer a need to have a military involvement in acquiring and protecting access to foreign oil

---

[1] Free primary energy and more efficient conversion saves $300 billion, trade deficit for oil $200 billion, it costs $100 billion to maintain the grid not counting the August 2003 blackout which cost $20 billion, subsidies to fossil/nuclear are $50 billion, clean up and remediation direct costs are $30 billion, externalities are at least $100 billion, the military cost for operations associated with oil are $100 billion per year.

In addition, the renewable energy economy would create $180 billion per year in new wealth after overhead, payroll, operation and maintenance costs are deducted from the value of the energy produced with the emerging technologies described in this book.

As an "economic strategy," a renewable energy based economy has at least a $930 billion per year advantage over the fossil/nuclear based economy[2].

Seven hundred and fifty billion dollars per year is currently wasted...lost to the purchase of foreign oil, lost to the inefficiency of coal-fired power[3], and tossed out as garbage[4] plus the many other expenses that we unnecessarily pay out with no economic return to the American public and their communities. By applying the $750 billion in avoided costs toward a renewable energy infrastructure, six million new jobs can be created, revitalizing communities all across America.

The obvious question then is: if one strategy pays back $930 billion, why hasn't this strategy been chosen by our leadership in the White House and Congress? Isn't it clear which plan benefits the American people the most?

The short answer is that corporations that benefit from the current way of doing things are able to exert a great deal of economic and political power, and at the same time, keep the average American in the dark through advertising and public relations efforts.

The strategies in this chapter make sense for the average American and for local economies across the country; they do not necessarily make sense for the oil, gas, nuclear, coal fired central generation based utilities, weapons and currently structured auto industries.

This chapter attempts to evaluate economic strategies using criteria that take into account all costs. It's as simple as that, **all costs.**

---

[2]Adding $750 billion to $180 billion gives a total of $930 billion per year.

[3]two-thirds of the energy in coal goes up the flue as wasted heat.

[4]18 quadrillion BTUs

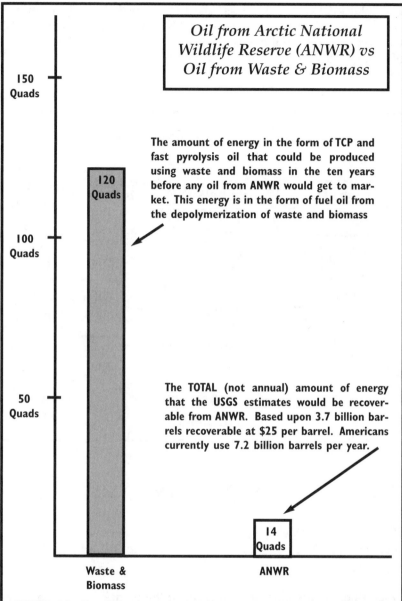

FIGURE 6.1 Two different strategies to acquire oil. The total amount of energy recoverable from the Arctic National Wildlife Refuge (ANWR) is dwarfed by the amount of oil that could be produced by the TCP and fast pyrolysis processes in the time it would take for the oil from ANWR to be brought to market, despite demands by the oil industry and certain politicians as to the necessity of drilling in the Arctic National Wildlife Refuge.

The "Quick Economic Analysis" chart can be used to analyze various energy conversion processes, such as TCP and fast pyrolysis, fuel cells, wind, coal fired central plants, nuclear, etc., in terms of either the flow of energy or the flow of money. There will always be an "input" and an "output" to evaluate.

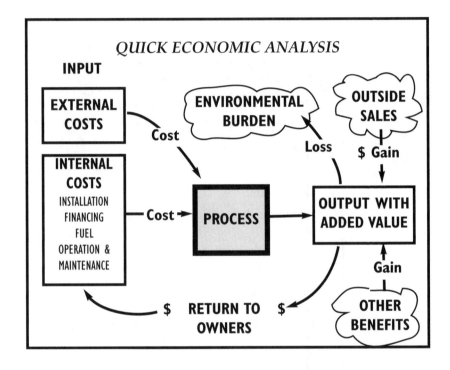

TCP PLANT ECONOMIC ANALYSIS

INTERNAL COSTS (Input)
Installation: The cost to build a 1000-ton per day TCP plant is $65 million.

Operation, maintenance and payroll for the plant costs $8 to $12 per barrel of oil produced or twenty to twenty-eight cents per gallon. A plant this size will employ about 100 people in $20 per hour jobs for a payroll of about $5 million per year.[5]

---

[5]Telephone conversation with Changing World Technologies, Inc., CEO, Brian Appel, April, 2004.

Fuel costs will vary depending on the feedstock, but if the plant takes toxic waste, municipal solid waste, plastic and used tires, it could conceivably operate with no fuel cost or even with feedstock tipping fees as a profit center. With a mix of feedstock, the tipping fees for some waste streams would pay to have local farmers deliver biomass at a rate of $50 to $75 per ton. If the plant took half biomass (150,000 tons per year), it would put $7.5 million to $11 million into the local economy as payments to family farms.

Financing. Based on a typical output of oil, the debt service for a ten year loan at 9% is $5 per barrel of oil or 12 cents per gallon.

EXTERNAL COSTS (Input)
With the TCP process, there are no emissions to the environment; the process is closed. With the TCP process, not only are there no external costs, waste related problems are often reduced or eliminated. Items -- such as feedlot waste, used tires, diseased livestock carcasses, used plastic, hospital waste and dangerous toxic wastes -- that were formerly a liability now become an asset.

ENVIRONMENTAL BURDEN (Deduct from Output)
As explained under the heading of externalities, there is no environmental burden since there are no emissions from the plant. Permitting the plants is not a problem, since they are defined as a manufacturing process, not a waste handling/disposal process.

OUTPUT
The typical TCP plant will produce over 22 million gallons of oil per year and add $60 million per year to the local economy -- $11 million in the form of payments to farm families per year, $15 million for plant payroll and another $33 for the sale of oil itself. This analysis does not take into account the other saleable by-products such as carbon, pure water and fertilizer grade minerals.

The net return to the owners is on the order of $8 to $10 million per year.

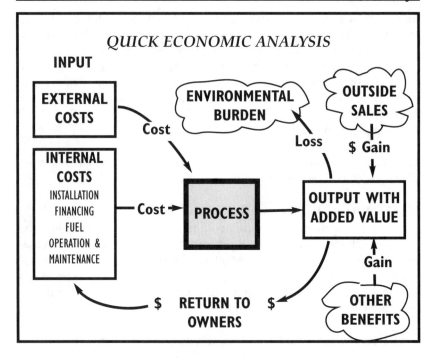

QUICK ECONOMIC ANALYSIS

HIGH TEMPERATURE FUEL CELLS
ECONOMIC ANALYSIS

INTERNAL COSTS (Input)

Installation: The installed cost for molten carbonate fuel cells (MCFC) is $1200 to $2000 per KW. SOFCs are in an earlier stage of development than MCFCs. There is a concerted effort on three continents to bring the manufacturing costs down. The projected cost according to the Department of Energy (DOE), which is coordinating research in the U.S., is for SOFCs to be at $400 per KW by 2010. Getting to $400 per KW depends on research and development dollars that become available and on some large orders to get the commercialization process under-way.

Operation and maintenance consists primarily of replacing the fuel cell stack every five years. The cost for this is about one fourth the original installed cost of the fuel cell. To be conservative, we use one-third the cost. For a twenty year life, this would require three stack replacements, giving a lifetime cost of two times the original installed cost.

Fuel costs vary of course. The high temperature fuel cells will use any hydrogen rich hydrocarbon, such as diesel fuel, TCP oil, fast pyrolysis "bio-oil," natural gas (methane), methanol, dimethyl ether, etc. See the sidebar chart (Figure 6.2) showing the fuel cell energy flow. For example, if the cost of natural gas is $6 per million BTUs, then the fuel cost component of the electricity is $.045 per kWh.

Financing fuel cells is much simpler than financing a large central fired plant, either coal or nuclear, because the fuel cell units are in identical modules. As many modules as necessary can be added, and they can be added whenever they are needed; there is no need to try to estimate and finance the capacity that will be needed far into the future. If more energy is needed, then more fuel cells can be added later. This also means that the fuel cells are operating at full capacity and high efficiency, as opposed to partial load and low efficiency. This also means that there is much less financial risk involved since many small, identical units are used instead of one extremely large plant.

EXTERNAL COSTS (Input)
The fuel cell can be considered as having no external costs associated with it. Carbon dioxide is produced if a hydrocarbon is used for fuel, but since there is no combustion and consequently no flue, the CO_2 is easily contained and sequestered, if necessary. The only other by-products are heat and chemically pure water.

OUTPUT
For high temperature fuel cells, the fuel to electricity efficiency is about 52% and about 40% of the input energy is recoverable heat, making the fuel cell up to 92% efficient. It does this quietly, so the units can be placed anywhere in a commercial building without interfering with tenant space. In addition, both the reliability and quality of the electricity is greater than for grid power. Since the unit is on site, the hot water can be conveniently recovered for space heating or domestic hot water.

Many high temperature fuel cell projects are being designed around alternative sources of fuel, such as methane from anaerobic digesters set up at sewage plants, methane that would normally escape from shaft coal mines and methane that would normally escape from surface coal beds. Another potential source of methane would be from gas and oil wells where the gas is entrained and must be sequestered (in the U.S.), or in other parts of the world where the methane is flared at the well. In these cases the methane is far lower in cost than $6 per million BTU, which would bring the cost of electricity down proportionally.

VALUE RETURNED TO OWNERS

On a community or industrial park level fuel cells could be installed to serve customers in the immediate area using underground cable. For example if fuel was available for $4 per million BTU, the fuel cost component of the electricity would be 2.6 cents. Add to that the installed cost of $800 per KW and operating and maintenance costs of $800 per KW over the 175,000 hour life of the system for one cent. This gives a cost of energy of 3.5 cents per kWh over the life of the system.

Note that the operating and maintenance and installation costs could be half that shown if the $400 per KW goal is reached. The lifetime of the system could also be in the range of 250,000 hours with periodic stack replacement. In this case the cost of energy would drop to below three cents per kWh which is lower than the best bulk commercial rates. Not counting inflation over the years and using current retail electric rates, the profit would still be five cents per kWh or $12,500 per installed KW, thirty times the initial investment and 16 times the investment including operating and maintenance costs. On an annual basis, the five cents per kWh totals over $400 which means that the payback is as short as one year on the initial cost, two years if operating and maintenance costs are included.

This analysis does not take into account the value of the recovered heat, which could lower the cost of electricity to below two cents per kWh if it was all recovered at $4 per million BTUs.

Another factor to take into account is that if the fuel cell installation were done on a community level where a TCP plant was already in operation, then the cost of fuel could drop to as low as $1.50 per million BTUs, lowering the cost of electricity accordingly.

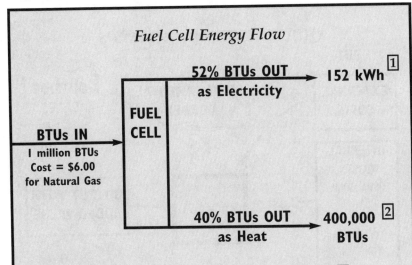

Fuel Cell Energy Flow

BTUs IN
1 million BTUs
Cost = $6.00
for Natural Gas

FUEL CELL

52% BTUs OUT as Electricity → 152 kWh [1]

40% BTUs OUT as Heat → 400,000 [2] BTUs

Cost of Electricity = 2.4 cents/kWh [3]

[1] Using natural gas, the cost for electricity from the Fuel Cell would be $.04/kWh using the following calculations:
520,000 BTUs/3412 BTUs/kWh = 152 kWh
$6.00/152 kWh = $.04/kWh

[2] If the heat is recovered, it is worth $6/M-BTUs or $2.40.

[3] If the value of the recovered heat is subtracted from the fuel cost ($6 minus $2.40), the adjusted cost for electricity is:
$3.60/152kWh = 2.4 cents/kWh using the formula
$/kWh = ($/M-BTU x .003412) divided by efficiency.

Note: This is fuel cost only. The true cost of electricity would also reflect the installation, operation and maintenance of the fuel cell, which for a SOFC would be between .5 and one cent per kWh.

FIGURE 6.2

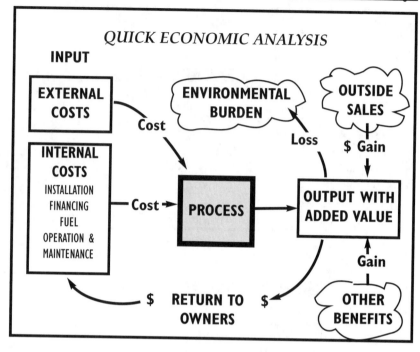

WIND ENERGY ECONOMIC ANALYSIS

INTERNAL COSTS (Input)

Installation of wind generators cost between $800 and $1000 per KW. Figuring a thirty year life and a capacity factor of 35%, the installed KW will generate a little more than three thousand kWh of electricity per year. This is about one cent per kWh.

Operation and maintenance of the wind generator amounts to about 1.2 cents per kWh over its life[6]. Operation of the wind farm includes such things as property taxes, land use fees, insurance, transmission and interconnect fees and management costs add up to about .4 cents per kWh. The maintenance costs, include all periodic maintenance as well as major overhauls on the turbine, come to about one cent per kWh.

---

[6]The operating cost per kWh would come to about 1.2 cents and typically break down accordingly: distribution and interconnects at .66 cents, operation and maintenance at .24 cents, payments for leasing and property taxes at .15 cents and management fees at .15 cents. Debt would vary but for a 15 year loan at 9.5% interest it would add about 1.8 cents. From The American Wind energy Association

Debt retirement is a major portion of the cost of wind energy and will typically add another 1 cent per kWh to the cost of energy.

EXTERNAL COSTS (Input)

There are no significant externalities associated with wind energy. By contrast, it should be noted that a recent study by the European Union shows that the externalities alone for coal fired electricity are between 3 and 6 cents per kWh, the same or double the production cost for wind energy. The externalities cited in the EU study do not include global warming.

OUTPUT

If the energy is marked up four cents per kWh, the revenue per MW of installed capacity is $122,000 per year, which is returned to the owners of the wind turbine. In Denmark, over two thirds of the wind turbines are owned by individuals or cooperatives as an investment. This trend is catching on in the U.S., especially in Minnesota where an additional state production tax credit is available to rural landowners to install wind power. The federal tax credit is 1.5 cents per kWh, but is dependent on inflation and is now at 1.8 cents. A difficulty with the production tax credit is that it must be renewed by an act of Congress every two years; this makes it difficult to plan large wind projects because of the uncertainty of the tax credit.

Other benefits of wind power are job creation, which is considered to be about one job per MW during construction and one permanent job per 20 MW thereafter. Studies in Europe show that there are between four and five jobs created indirectly for every installed MW. A New York state study indicated that wind creates 27% more jobs than comparable capacity in coal fired generation and 66% more jobs than natural gas fired power.

Revenues from wind accrue to the owners who pay the county government in the form of taxes; in Minnesota this amounts to about $4700 per MW per year, and other states report on the order of 1-1.4% of the investment going to property taxes.

Leasing arrangements with landowners pay between $2500 and $3,000 per MW per year or as much as 4% of the gross revenues, depending on the type of contract the landowner enters into.

ADDING VALUE TO WASTE

This illustration (Figure 6.3) uses four different processes to add value to 138 pounds of waste material. Notice how the waste, which contains 1 million BTUs to begin with, loses some of its energy content with each stage that it passes through but the BTUs that are contained in the output, even though there are fewer of them, have a greater value than before they entered the process. TCP turns the waste into carbon and oil. The carbon is put through another process called "activation" which subjects it to very high temperature and pressure steam turning what was carbon black into a valuable filtration medium called activated carbon. The oil can be either sold on the open market or used to fire a SOFC which in turn generates electricity and hot water at over 1000 degrees F. The hot water can be further processed through a turbine and generator in a process called "combined cycle" to make more electricity.

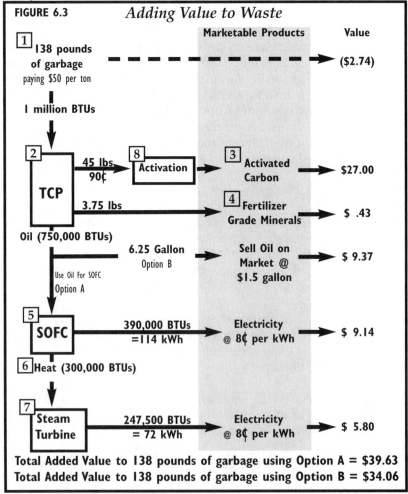

FIGURE 6.3   *Adding Value to Waste*

Total Added Value to 138 pounds of garbage using Option A = $39.63
Total Added Value to 138 pounds of garbage using Option B = $34.06

Notes to Figure 6.3

1. Garbage --municipal solid waste, sewage sludge, used tires, diseased cattle, etc. -- is fed into the macerator at the local TCP plant where the process depolymerizes it and converts it to oil and other by-products. For illustration purposes, we assume that we are willing to pay $50 per ton for the garbage. A ton of garbage has about 16 million BTUs; this works out to $2.74 per million BTUs.

2. The TCP plant converts 75% of the input BTUs to oil and can make 6.25 gallons out of a million BTUs of garbage at a cost of 40 cents per gallon; this amounts to $2.50 or $3.33 per million BTUs. The oil could be sold at retail in the same community that makes it for $1.50 per gallon, giving the million BTUs a value of $9.37. Road taxes, etc. are not paid on the oil for this illustration. The oil could also be sold for input into high temperature fuel cells within the community, in which case it would be marked up from the 40 cent cost to $1 per gallon with profits going to the plant operator. At a dollar a gallon, the oil is now worth $6.25, about the same as natural gas, depending on the current price, which could range up to $10 per million BTUs. This illustrates an important point: the price of garbage is much more stable than the price of natural gas.

3. Carbon black is a by-product of the TC process, see note eight.

4. Fertilizer grade minerals are a by-product of the TC process; they could be sold in bulk at about $250 per ton or 43 cents worth for the million BTU input to the plant.

5. The fuel cell produces electricity at 52% efficiency from fuel input BTUs to BTUs in the form of electrical energy [see Figure 6.2]. After the conversion loss of 25% of the garbage BTUs, we are able to input 750,000 BTUs in the form of oil into the solid oxide fuel cell (SOFC). This input energy results in 114 kWh of electricity, which is worth $9.14 at a retail rate of 8 cents per kWh.

6. A by-product of the fuel cell is heat in the form of hot water; we can recover 40% of the input BTUs in this form, or 300,000 BTUs. These BTUs are worth $6 per million, or $1.80.

7. As an option to using the hot water for space heating, it can be used as input into a steam turbine, which in turn is connected to a generator. This arrangement, called combined cycle generation, will increase the fuel to electricity efficiency to over 80% giving another $5.80 worth of electrical energy. Again, this is figured at a retail rate of 8 cents per kWh. Adding this electricity to the 114 kWh gives a total of $14.94 worth of electricity.

8. Carbon black is worth about 2-4 cents per pound, but it can be activated and turned into a much more valuable by-product. Activated carbon is worth up to $1 per pound, figure 75 cents per pound and deduct 15 cents per pound for the activation process for a net value for the carbon of $27. This calculation is based on the amount of carbon that would be produced per million BTUs of input into the TC process.

AN ECONOMIC STRATEGY FOR A TYPICAL COUNTY

Here's how the strategy would work: Assume that the county owns and operates the TCP plant, the 57 MW of high temperature fuel cells and the 160 MW of wind turbines cooperatively and in turn sells the electricity and some oil (8.3 million gallons) to the residents of the county. Investors and residents can participate in the co-op much the way it is done in Denmark today with wind generation (see Figure 6.4).

The county contracts with 200 drivers to deliver 1000 tons of waste and biomass per day to the county TCP plant. In this simplified example the drivers are paid $60,000 per year, in reality the county contracts would have to reflect the use of heavy garbage trucks vs drivers using their own one ton pickups to haul biomass and agricultural waste. The cost to the county is $13.5 million; this reflects overhead expenses of $2.7 million, and net feedstock payments of $6 million. For some feedstock, the TCP plant is able collect a tipping fee, which will offset the overall cost of feedstock.

The TCP plant produces 22.5 million gallons of oil per year, which is owned by the county. Some oil is sold directly to residents at the co-op filling station (8.3 million gallons), and the rest is used to fire the SOFCs in order to produce electricity and heat, which will is sold on the open market.

The 57 MW of fuel cell capacity is divided into a variety of units sized to serve single residences (1 KW), commercial buildings and schools (10- 250 KW) up to large units designed to serve entire commercial districts (10 MW). The county owns and maintains the fuel cells and sells the electricity and heat at retail prices. The fuel cells require a total of 14.2 million gallons of TCP oil and are able to generate 500 million kWh of electricity, half of the electrical demand for the county. This operation employs about 150 people with a payroll of $5.4 million. An additional $1.2 million per year in expenses is required for stack replacement for the fuel cells.

The other 500 million kWh of electricity is furnished with wind, requiring 160 MW of installed capacity and employing 15 people at $36,000 per year for a payroll of $540,000. The wind is considered the base load with the fuel cells furnishing electricity on demand, which is to say when the wind isn't blowing. This illustration is simplified in that 50% may be pushing the limits of a workable wind contribution to the electrical mix, depending on how much diversity there is in the demand load.

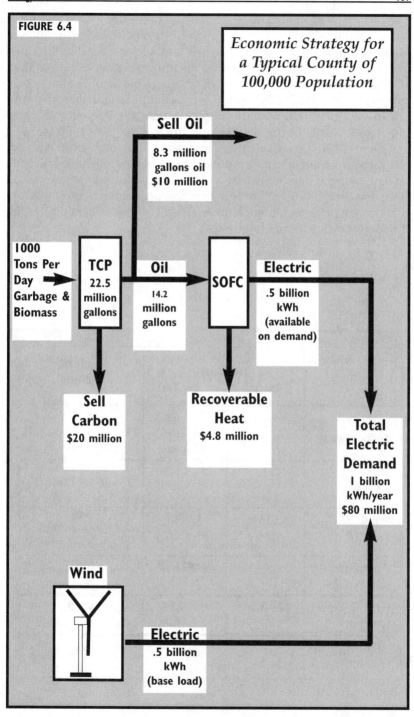

FIGURE 6.4

Economic Strategy for a Typical County of 100,000 Population

The county takes in $110 million in energy and carbon sales and pays out $21 million in salaries, which stays in the county. The county has found 50 million it didn't have before, and all for a $24.2 million per year payment (for ten years) to fund the infrastructure. Four hundred sixty-five jobs are created as a result of being able to add value to primary energy (waste, biomass and wind) that is acquired locally and processed locally. The primary energy is essentially free, instead of letting it go to waste the county is using it to generate wealth. Please note that there is a **NET** increase in jobs, if someone loses their job in the next county because the utility went out of business, they will be able to continue working at the county level and continue to be in the energy business. Incidentally, 57 MW of fuel cells is a large enough order to justify putting a manufacturing plant, or at least a final assembly plant, in the county, creating even more jobs.

	Cost (Millions)		Benefit (Millions)
	Install	Per Year	
TCP **1000 ton/day**	$65	$2.7 O&M $6 Feed $4.8 Haul	**$10** (Sell 8.3 million gallons @ $1.20) **$20** (Sell carbon)
SOFC **57 MW**	$23	$1.2 O&M	**$40** (Sell 500 M kWh @ eight cents kWh)
Wind **160 MW**	$144	$7 O&M	**$40** (Sell 500 M kWh @ eight cents kWh)
Payroll for **465 People**		$21	**465 Jobs**
First Ten Years **(per year)**	$24.2 debt	$44.7	**$110**
Following Years **(per year)**		$44.7	**$110**

FIGURE 6.5

AN ECONOMIC STRATEGY FOR AMERICA

On the floor of the Senate in October 2003, Senator James Inhoffe of Oklahoma is quoted as proclaiming, ..."global warming is the biggest scam ever perpetrated on the American people."

Among those who know better than that, and have stated so, are members of his own Pentagon, the global insurance industry and the oil industry.[7]

There are those who will proclaim desperately that attempting to transition the entire U.S. economy from one based on fossil fuel and nuclear energy to one based on renewable energy is too costly and impractical.

Those who know better understand that a renewable energy economy is both workable and preferable. The reasons why this is true cannot be stated too emphatically or frequently, so we'll repeat them here:

- The primary energy is free...waste, wind, sun and ocean movement

- A great deal of inefficiency and waste is eliminated

- There is no clean up required

- There is no more need for welfare or giveaways to mature industries...to say nothing of polluting industries

- There are no externalities to pay

- The federal trade deficit is reduced considerably

- The need for an electrical transmission grid is reduced considerably

- The need for military involvement in energy acquisition and protection is eliminated, resulting in a stronger national defense.

- There is less government involvement and, therefore, less tax, less regulation and less government spending

- There is greater opportunity for "free market" capitalism to flourish

---

[7]See Chapter Two, page 90-91.

CLEAN ENERGY FOR AMERICA

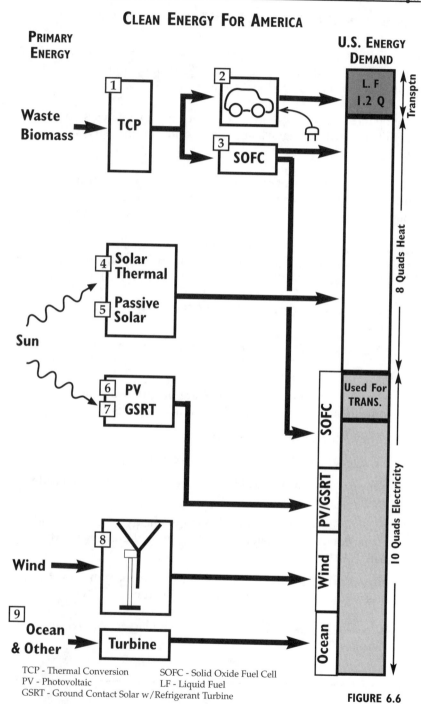

PRIMARY ENERGY

U.S. ENERGY DEMAND

Waste Biomass

1 TCP

2 (car)

3 SOFC

4 Solar Thermal
5 Passive Solar

Sun

6 PV
7 GSRT

Wind

8

9 Ocean & Other Turbine

L. F 1.2 Q — Transptn

8 Quads Heat

Used For TRANS.

SOFC

PV/GSRT

Wind

Ocean

10 Quads Electricity

TCP - Thermal Conversion   SOFC - Solid Oxide Fuel Cell
PV - Photovoltaic   LF - Liquid Fuel
GSRT - Ground Contact Solar w/Refrigerant Turbine

FIGURE 6.6

Figure 6.4 shows graphically how the energy flows through a U.S. renewable energy economy. The essential underlying facts are that we have five times more primary energy than we need, and it is renewed over and over again each year. We have the technology to do it now, either available or very close to it. We have the money to fund this strategy ten times over (Chapter 7) without costing the average taxpayer (under $200,000 per year income) a cent.

1. Three thousand TCP plants will be built, each with a capacity of 1000 tons per day. They will produce 85 billion gallons of fuel oil. The principle by-product from the TCP plants is carbon black, which can be activated and sold for up to $1 per pound. The fuel oil is used in both the PDHEVs and high temperature fuel cells.

2. A direct subsidy of $15,000 will go to 10 million people for ten years for the purchase of a full sized plug-in diesel hybrid electric vehicle (PDHEV). The fleet of 100 million PDHEVs will cover the 3 trillion mile U.S. demand using 10 billion gallons of #2 fuel oil from the TCP plants for 20% of the miles and .65 trillion kWh of electricity for 80% of the miles traveled.

3. An installed capacity of 160,000 MW of solid oxide fuel cells (SOFC) will be put in place on site (no grid required) to produce both electricity and hot water using 75 billion gallons of fuel oil from the TCP plants as fuel. Half of the hot water heat will be recovered for space heating and domestic hot water, furnishing 1.6 Q (20%) toward the 8 Q demand. 1.38 trillion kWh of electricity will be produced, this is 46% of the total electrical demand for the U.S.

4. Eighty percent of the space heating and DHW demand, 6.4 Q, will be furnished using a mix of solar thermal installations and passive solar retrofits. This will require 40 billion square feet (SF) of solar thermal collector.

5. One hundred million passive heating retrofits will be installed.

6. No photovoltaic collectors will be used in this strategy.

7. Solar electricity will be generated using a ground mounted solar collector and refrigerant/gas turbine and generator (GSRT) configuration. This system will require 40 billion SF of collector area for an installed capacity of 144,200 MW to generate .72 trillion kWh which is 24% of total demand.

8. Wind energy will provide .66 trillion kWh, 22% of demand, using 215,000 MW of installed capacity.

9. Ocean turbines and a host of other alternative methods of generating clean electricity will be used. This strategy will call for 34,000 MW of submerged, open center type turbines in the Gulf Stream off the east coast of the U.S. This method will account for 8% of the total demand of 3 trillion kWh, or .24 trillion kWh.

Clean Energy For America Costs and Benefits

	Approximate Cost	Some Benefits
1. TCP	3000 plants at $65 M each= $19.5 B per year over ten years	Retail value for 85 B gallons of oil at $1.20 is $102 B per year, carbon sales in the tens of billions of dollars. 300,000 permanent jobs, 600,000 construction jobs.
2. PDHEV	A direct subsidy to 10 M new car buyers at $15,000 each is $150 B per year	Net fuel savings of $180 B per year (includes the additional electrical costs for the PDHEVs)
3. SOFCs	160,000 MW installed at $400 per KW is $6.4 B per year for ten years. Operation and maintenance for the ten years is another $4.2 B for $10.6 B per year	The 1.38 trillion kWh retails at $110 B per year
4. Solar thermal	40 B square feet of collector would cost $100 B for ten years as a 50% rebate to homeowners.	3.2 Q of heat would be worth about $16 B per year at $5 per M BTU rate. Millions of jobs would be created for the installation
5. Passive solar	Subsidizing half the cost for 100 M passive additions would cost $100 B per year for ten years	3.2 Q of heat would be worth about $16 B per year. Millions of jobs would be created for the construction of the additions
6. PV	Not used in this strategy	
7. GSRT	144,200 MW would be installed for $12 B per year for ten years	720 B kWh of electricity retails for $57 B per year
8. WIND	215,000 MW would cost $20 B per year for ten years	660 B kWh of electricity would retail for $52 B per year. 10,000 permanent jobs would be created.
9. OCEAN	34,000 MW of capacity would be installed at a cost of $4 B per year for ten years	240 B kWh of electricity would retail for $19 B per year
TOTAL first ten years	Cost to install is $416 B per year for ten years. An interest free loan or gift is required in the amount $236 B per year for ten years.	Return is $552 B per year gross, $180 B per year after payroll, operation and maintenance
TOTAL after ten years	The renewable energy infrastructure is installed	The return is $180 B per year

FIGURE 6.7

With this economic strategy in place, one hundred million people will be driving a new PDHEV, have solar thermal collectors and a passive solar addition on their homes. Over six million new jobs will have been created and the trade deficit will have been cut in half. There will be no more black outs, no more toxic waste or feedlot stench and no need to recycle. Everyone will be safer and 2.3 billion tons per year of carbon dioxide will not be dumped into the atmosphere.

Not included in the benefits column are numerous avoided costs, money that is now being spent that would be immediately available to be transferred back to the taxpayer and put toward other useful social purposes, such as health care or education -- or it could be applied directly into paying down the installation costs of the renewable energy economy.

Clean Energy For America Costs and Benefits Infrastructure Only

	Cost to Install	Retail Value of Production
TCP	3000 at $65 M each = $195 Billion	$227 Billion Oil and Carbon
SOFCs	160,000 MW installed at $400 per KW = $64 Billion	$110 Billion Electric $ 64 Billion Heat
GSRT	144,200 MW = $120 Billion	$57 Billion Electric
WIND	215,000 MW = $200 Billion	$52 Billion Electric
OCEAN	340,000 MW = $40 Billion	$19 Billion Electric
TOTAL	$619 Billion	$529 Billion per year

FIGURE 6.8 The installed costs represents infrastructure that will be in place for 30 years. The value of production energy and goods is for one year. Operation, maintenance, overhead, payroll and financing costs must be deducted from the value of the produced goods and energy services, but the payback is still very short...less than ten years.

The old ways of acquiring energy are dirty, unsafe and expensive. The avoided costs associated with the items below are reflected in the surprisingly good economics shown by Figure 6.8 above.

•With the current system, an enormous amount of energy is simply wasted...unnecessarily

• Subsidies and giveaways now in place are largely going to the wrong people, mature polluting industries

• Large quantities of U.S. dollars are now flowing out of the country to purchase primary energy...unnecessarily

• The U.S. now maintains certain expensive infrastructure when, for the most part, it is not needed...such as the electric grid

• Currently, there are huge unaccounted expenditures to pay for externalities, such as global warming and mercury emissions that could be eliminated.

Conclusion: The U.S. has five times as much clean, renewable primary energy as it needs. Using it, instead of fossil fuels and nuclear would create millions of jobs, revitalize communities all across America, reduce the federal trade deficit, make us all safer and result in an environmental legacy of which we could be proud. Not only do we have the energy necessary to transition to a renewable energy economy, the funding is available ten times over to make the transition, as we'll explore in the next chapter.

Fun with Energy

Following are some miscellaneous ideas and strategies regarding energy. They are here for balance and to remind us that a seemingly preposterous suggestion, such as powering southern California on seaweed, is not only economically feasible, but when analyzed honestly, it is probably a much better idea than importing LNG from Bolivia, for example, especially when the people of California are being shackled with a long term contract to purchase a foreign fossil fuel at a certain price.

Perhaps it's worth taking a moment to pause and think which is more outlandish, traveling 7000 miles on restaurant grease or throwing away a fuel containing 150,000 BTUs of clean energy per gallon? Which choice really makes more sense, purchasing our energy from a North Dakota farmer...or a Saudi prince?

Powering Southern California on Seaweed

This strategy proposes to furnish the transportation fuel for southern California with seaweed. Here's how.

Brown algae (*Macrocystis pyrifera*) is a common sight washed up on the beaches of California. It grows at an extremely rapid rate in the open ocean having fronds several hundred feet long and requiring no fertilization, no herbicides and no land. It is estimated that the yields of kelp could be in the range of 50 dry tons per acre if it were grown in managed kelp farms off the California coast. This is in contrast to corn, for example, which would yield 6 to 8 tons per acre and require land to do it, of course.

It is known that kelp can be harvested with specially equipped ships by first anchoring the fronds to plastic grids below the ocean surface. A project conducted in the 1970s and 1980s by the American Gas Association, the Gas Research Institute, the U.S. Department of Energy and the Department of the Navy studied the possibility of using kelp to supply biomass to be used as a source of methane through anaerobic digestion in case the price of natural gas became too high.[8] The techniques for growing and harvesting the kelp were developed under this project. The project was discontinued in the late 1980s, but it was discovered that kelp is a likely source of biomass.

If only PDHEVs were in use in southern California, the liquid fuel requirement to go 360 billion miles would be six billion gallons of fuel (60 mpg for the 20% of mileage using the diesel engine of the PDHEV). At a TCP production rate of 70 gallons of fuel per ton of biomass, it would require 100 million tons of biomass per year, and at a harvest rate of 50 tons per acre, it would require two million acres of ocean surface or an area 56 miles by 56 miles.

If the fossil crude oil is currently imported into the state, then the six billion gallons of TCP oil from seaweed represents $10 billion that remains in the state of California.

---

[8]Klass, Donald L. *Biomass For Renewable Energy, Fuels and Chemicals*. Academic Press, London. 1998:486-7. Kelp yield data is taken from Bryce, A. J. *Energy From Biomass and Wastes*. 1978.

CROSS-COUNTRY ON RESTAURANT GREASE

This strategy illustrates Buckminister Fuller's admonition that "pollution is nothing but the resources we are not harvesting. We allow them to disburse because we've been ignorant of their value." If used grease is clean, non-toxic, free and has a greater volumetric energy content than diesel fuel, what sense does it make to throw it away? Yet, that is exactly what we do....three million tons of used grease per year.

In order to convert a diesel vehicle to run on grease or straight vegetable oil (SVO)[9], a kit can be purchased for about $500, which includes the fittings, valves and heaters necessary to run on SVO. The vehicle needs to start on regular diesel and then switch over to SVO, so two tanks are required, as well as a tank heater for the SVO in order to prevent it from gelling in cold weather. The SVO itself needs to be filtered in order to take out the food particles.

SVO is considered a fuel equivalent of fossil diesel and may even be better in terms of engine wear with its superior lubricity. Grease is extremely energy dense, with well over the 128,400 BTU per gallon of fossil diesel.

SVO is the perfect end use energy carrier. It is non-toxic, easy to transport, easy to store in bulk, easy to store on board the vehicle; it has a very high gravimetric energy content (20,000 BTU per pound); it has great volumetric energy content (180,000 BTU per gallon which incidentally, is better than gasoline or diesel); and it's free.

Restaurant grease has, in the past, been treated as unwanted waste to be disposed of at a cost. The economic realities are becoming apparent with the increasing difficulty in obtaining free restaurant grease, and with the scarcity of old model VW diesel vehicles available in the used auto/truck market. Running diesel vehicles on restaurant grease is becoming a popular thing to do.

Anyone fortunate enough to find a used diesel vehicle and willing to collect 500 gallons of used grease per year can become transportation fuel self-sufficient. Look for states to take notice and begin to demand road taxes on the restaurant grease.

SVO exhaust is low in nitrous oxides and has no sulfur, making it extremely clean burning. Since the oil is originally made from plants,

---

[9]SVO and grease are the same thing except that grease has been used for cooking and must be filtered.

it is carbon neutral, so greenhouse gases do not accumulate in the atmosphere (see Figure 2.11)

The U.S. throws away 970 million gallons of used grease per year. These two enterprising, recent graduates of Gustavus Adolphus College (Minnesota) used about 200 gallons of it to fuel their 7000 mile, cross-country adventure. Aaron Crowell (above left) and Phil Graeve (right), advocates for the environment, converted a 1981 Volkswagen diesel truck to run on used restaurant grease. The conversion cost $500 and took them about a week to install, although neither are expert mechanics. Phil (bottom left) strains grease prior to "filling up" using their giant "bucket funnel" (arrow below right). Aaron reports that, "the best quality fuel came from Japanese sushi restaurants, although some pizza places had pretty good stuff."

Buying Wind Energy From
The Good Citizens of North and South Dakota

This strategy proposes to purchase 22% of the nation's electrical energy from the citizens of North and South Dakota who are blessed with a superb natural resource....similar to the 5000 or so princes of the House of Saud who have been living lavishly off the Saudi oil revenues their entire lives.

Twenty two percent of the total U.S. electrical demand would be met with wind energy from North and South Dakota -- less than half of the wind energy capacity of these two states. In this scenario, the states of North and South Dakota would receive a federal loan guarantee for $215 billion for 60,000 wind generators of 3.6 MW capacity each.

Over the thirty-year life of the units, the production would be 20 trillion kWh of electrical energy having a retail value (at $.08 per kWh) without inflation, of $1.6 trillion. The energy would be sold wholesale for $.04 per kWh for total revenue of $800 billion. In addition to paying off the interest free loan and the operating and maintenance costs, the people of North and South Dakota would have to be compensated for their inconvenience. This strategy proposes that those who have a wind generator on their land be paid a leasing fee of $10,000 per year per unit. In addition, every person over the age of 18 would be paid $2000 per year, tax free. These payments would amount to less than one cent per kWh.

Three and a half acres per wind generator would be taken out of agricultural production; this includes access roads and siting. On average, there would be one unit per 1500 acres, although the wind energy potential for the states only takes into account land that is within 20 miles of the grid, non-urban, and avoid sensitive environmental and wildlife areas.

COWS TO OIL

This strategy proposes that slaughterhouse remains and diseased cattle be converted into oil and other valuable by-products by processing with the TCP technology.

In the U.S., there are 500,000 "downer cows" per year. These are cows that are weakened or diseased to the point of not being able to stand up and are now being rendered into other products such as animal food. In addition, 35 million cows are slaughtered each year in the U.S., of which 50% of the cow is rendered. Together, this amounts to 8.2 million tons of cow remains and does not include other animals such as hogs, poultry, etc.

Similar feedstock is currently being used at the Carthage, Missouri plant and is producing 100 gallons of a light #2 fuel oil per ton, in addition to about 60 pounds of fertilizer grade minerals and 700 pounds of carbon. The 8.2 million tons of cow created in the U.S. would produce 820 million gallons of fuel oil, 224,000 tons of fertilizer grade minerals and 5 billion pounds of carbon black.

In some cases, slaughterhouse waste is a liability that costs money for disposal; some of it has a minimal value and is sold to a rendering plant to be made into animal food. Because of the controversy surrounding mad cow disease (bovine spongeform encephalopathy), it may soon be illegal to use this waste for feed, in which case, it would become even more of a liability.

The value of the products would be roughly as follows:

- 820 million gallons of oil at $1.50 = $1.23 billion
- 224,000 tons of minerals at $250 per ton = $56 million
- 5 billion pounds of carbon at 60 cents per pound after the cost to activate it = $3 billion

The total value of the products for a year comes to over $4 billion.

Twenty-three thermal conversion process (TCP) plants would be required, each with a capacity of 1000 tons per day, at a cost per plant of $65 million. The cost to install, maintain, operate and amortize the debt over ten years is $345 million per year for all 23 plants.

Considering the value of the oil only at $1 billion per year, the plants would make a profit of $650 million per year after paying all capital and operating costs.

One plant would support about 100 full-time positions at about $20 per hour. In addition, there would be construction and a multiplier effect in the community with $40 million worth of oil alone being produced and sold locally.

The 820 million gallons of oil from these plants would decrease the federal trade deficit by over $1 billion per year.

7 A Matter of Choice

It is not a question of making the choice or not making the choice. The question is **who** will make the choice...if we don't do it, someone else will. If the choices continue to be made by corporations who, in effect, determine the energy policy of the U.S., then we will continue with economic strategies that serve those interests over the interests of the average American.

The term "subsidy" is often misunderstood. A subsidy is supposed to be money that is disbursed as legitimate aid to a promising, emerging industry to help it get on the track to full-scale commercialization. Such a strategy is good policy and helps everyone; the nation, the economy and the entrepreneurs. Unfortunately, all too often subsidies are misused and are actually money that is handed to mature, profitable industries as a political payoff. Welfare to the rich is not subsidizing ...it's looting. The litmus test should be whether or not the money will be repaid in the form of economic wealth to the public, i.e. the taxpayers, from where it came.

Make no mistake, the transition of the U.S. to a renewable energy economy is an investment that has an astounding and immediate payback. The transition may need a loan or investment subsidy to put renewable energy into place quickly, but it pays for itself in record time. There are very good reasons why a transition of this nature has a good payback. They include these facts, repeated once again:

- The primary energy is free

- There is a far more efficient use of energy both in converting primary energy and using energy

- There are no clean up costs…in fact some processes clean up existing messes

- There are no more subsidies to profitable, polluting, politically connected industries

- There is no need for a military involvement

- There is a much reduced need for the electrical grid

- There are far fewer expensive externalities

The foregoing facts account for huge amounts of wasted money as well as wasted energy. Twice as much money is wasted per year on the seven items above than it would cost to implement a total and complete transition to a renewable energy economy. The benefits of a renewable energy economy would be

- millions of new jobs

- revitalized local economies all across the country

- a reduced trade deficit

- increased national security

- an environmental legacy of which we can be proud

It's a matter of choice. The majority of the American public has no idea of the kinds of freeewheeling spending that has been going on in Washington, D.C. and the choices policy makers have been making that affect our future. Here is but a small sampling of some choices that could be made differently.

A Matter of Choice

In general the list on the left shows subsidies that could have been, economic winners that would have a payback had they been funded. The items listed on the right could be thought of as economic losers, a waste that reflects the result of allowing the fossil/nuclear and weapons industries to make federal policy. Many of the abuses on the right can be stopped or reversed with leaders and policy makers who are willing to do so.

If You Could Choose	
A OR	**B**
$206 billion Cost per year for 13 million people to be given a $15,000 direct subsidy to purchase a full sized plug in diesel hybrid electric vehicle (PDHEV)	**$206 billion** Annual U.S. trade deficit for the purchase of foreign oil
$214 Billion $12 Billion fuel costs using PDHEVs $52 Billion electric costs PDHEVs $150 Billion subsidy to encourage purchases of PDHEVs	**$233 Billion** Amount spent at the pump on gasoline and diesel now
$2 billion Enough money to install 5000 MW of high temperature fuel cells in Iraq, this would supply the entire demand for the country plus give them free heating and clean water as a by-product	**$2 billion** Cost for one year, not including military protection and escort, to provide Iraqi citizens with 5 cent per gallon gasoline in order to mollify them
$3.4 billion Money to fund all basic research, all development and all pre-commercialization costs for every form of emerging renewable energy technology mentioned in this book	**$3.4 billion** Annual cost to U.S. taxpayer, through the Price-Anderson Act, to pay for insuring nuclear power plants against claims in the case of accident
$61 million The total 2004 budget for wind energy research at the National Renewable Energy Laboratory (NREL)	**$61 million** Amount that Halliburton admitted to overcharging the pentagon for gasoline not hauled from Kuwait to Iraq

IF YOU COULD CHOOSE

A   OR   B

A	B
$100 million Cost to install a 110 MW wind farm. This would generate electricity for 42,000 homes for the next 30 years	**$100 million** The amount that the pentagon was charged for airline tickets that were purchased but not used since March 2003. Refunds could have been granted but no one at the pentagon bothered to request them
$6 billion Amount of money to purchase outright 150,000 luxury, full sized PDHEVs	**$6 billion** Amount allocated for research and development on nuclear weapons in the 2004 budget
$18 billion Amount of money to purchase outright another 450,000 luxury, full sized PDHEVs	**$18 billion** Unaccounted for money in Iraq spending. Thought to be used as bribes to members of the "coalition of the willing"
$1 billion The amount required to put 83,000 Iraqi people to work installing high temperature fuel cells in their country	**$1 billion** Amount spent between May and October 2003 to look for weapons of mass destruction in Iraq after U.N inspectors reported that there were none
$18 billion Loan guarantee required to install flat plate, hot water solar thermal collectors on 8 million homes	**$18 billion** Loan guarantee (U.S. taxpayer) for a gas pipeline from Alaska to the Chicago area
$131 million Represents 2.8 times more than the Bush administration requested to secure U.S. ports against terrorist attack in 2005. Bush requested $46 million, the Coast Guard asked for $7.5 billion over ten years	**$131 million** Amount proposed in legislation to protect the Caño Limon pipeline in Colombia (for one year) for the benefit of Occidental Petroleum, this equals $3.58 per barrel of oil

IF YOU COULD CHOOSE	
A OR	**B**
$214 million This would install 180 MW of high temperature fuel cells at current costs, enough electricity to power and partially heat 156,000 homes	**$214 million** Spending on air bases in Alaska which was unrequested. Note: Ted Stevens (R-AK) is chairman of the Senate Appropriations Committee
$75 billion The amount required to build 1100 thousand ton per day TCP plants in the U.S. that would produce more oil from waste and biomass than the U.S. imports from the Middle East	**$75 billion** Amount per year, not including Iraq, that it costs for military involvement in protecting foreign oil supplies
$100 million Sixty percent more than the Department of Energy has funded NREL to improve wind energy extraction techniques	**$100 million** Annual Department of Energy (DOE) subsidies to the oil industry to improve oil extraction techniques
$1 billion Enough money to electrify 55,000 villages in the third world, using PV systems, where they currently have no electricity	**$1 billion** Amount spent per year according to pollster John Zogby by the U.S. to improve its image abroad
$611 billion Enough money to install 342,000 MW of SOFC capacity. This much capacity would generate ALL of the electricity and ALL of the residential and commercial space heat and domestic hot water for the U.S. (calculated at $900 per installed KW which is twice the project cost in seven years)	**$611 billion** $66 billion. Amount given to the nuclear industry to date for research and development $145 billion. Amount given to the nuclear industry to date in subsidies $400 billion. Estimated cost to decommission the existing nuclear power plants in the U.S.

IF YOU COULD CHOOSE

A OR B	
$36 billion Enough money to install a renewable energy infrastructure in 140 counties. This would employ 113,000 people and put $18 billion per year directly into the local communities	**$36 billion** Handouts and subsidies to oil, gas and nuclear corporations in pending bill [HR-4] House of Representatives
$50 billion Enough to purchase 42 billion gallons of TCP oil in 3000 counties, or $14 million per county	**$50 billion** The profit in 2002 from four major oil companies
$8 billion The amount of money required to subsidize 390 billion kWh of electrical power with the Production Tax Credit which is currently 1.8 cents per kWh. 390 billion kWh is 13% of U.S. demand	**$8 Billion** $1 billion equals the amount to be given by taxpayers to the nuclear industry in recent (July 2004) tax reform package for decommissioning $7 billion equals the amount in same tax package to be given to oil/gas/coal corporations as tax breaks
$1.3 billion This would pay for 86,000 of the $15,000 subsidies for new car buyers to purchase a PDHEV, resulting in a savings of 166 million gallons of fuel per year	**$1.3 billion** The amount of money lost to the U.S. treasury from the $100,000 per vehicle tax write-offs for the Hummer type vehicles, as of November 2003
$80 million Payroll for 2000 people to work at local TCP plants at $40,000 per year	**$80 million** Money being rebated to millionaire members of Bush's cabinet in the Bush tax rebate
$32 billion The amount required to install 35,000 MW of wind generation	**$32 billion** Amount loaned on fossil energy projects by Export-Import Bank and OPIC in the past ten years

IF YOU COULD CHOOSE

A	OR	B

A	B
$3.2 billion Amount of money to install renewable energy infrastructure (TCP, SOFC, Wind) in 12 locations @ $255 million. This would bring in $1.5 billion in revenue per year and employ 10,000 people	**$3.2 billion** Value of the tax breaks offered to Boeing by the State of Washington to entice the corporation to put the new 7E7 plant in Seattle and create 1200 jobs. That's $2.7 million per job
$15 billion Would pay for the 1.8 cent/kWh Production Tax Credit (PTC) for wind energy to furnish 28% of the total U.S. electrical energy demand	**$15 billion** Loan guarantees from the U.S. taxpayer (Senate bill-14) to the nuclear industry in addition to a guarantee to buy the power back. The beneficiaries are Dominion Energy, Exelon Corp and Entergy who collectively had $33.4 billion in revenues in 2002
$65 million Amount required to build a 1,000 ton per day TCP or fast pyrolysis plant	**$64.62 million** $49,700,000 The difference in taxpayer money between the bid from an Iraqi Engineering firm ($300,000) to rebuild a bridge in Baghdad and the winning bid from an American firm to do the work ($50 million). $14,920,000 The difference in money between the amount awarded to an American firm ($15 million) and actual cost to build a cement factory by an Iraqi firm ($80,000). The American firm was prevented by delays from building it so the Iraqi firm went ahead with the project

IF YOU COULD CHOOSE	
A OR	**B**
$140 billion The largest onshore wind project in the world is in Iowa. Enough money to install 325 of such wind projects which would supply 13% of U.S. electricity for the next 30 years	**$140 billion** Airline bailout of 2002
$70 billion The amount of money required to build a GSRT system large enough to provide electricity to 42 million homes (1/3 of all homes in the U.S.) for 30 years	**$70 billion** $20 billion equals the estimated costs to refurbish Iraqi pipelines $50 billion equals the amount that Exxon-Mobil will spend in the next five years to find and develop new oil fields
$36 billion Enough money to install a renewable energy infrastructure in 140 counties. This would employ 113,000 people and put $18 billion per year directly into the local communities	**$36 billion** Amount offered to Turkey for allowing U.S. troops to stage there in March 2003. Turkish parliament declined the offer (bribe)
108.5 billion Would install 1670 TCP plants and employ 180,000 people for twenty years	**108.5 billion** Spent to date (2 years) for Homeland Security, the largest government agency in history with 180,000 employees

IF YOU COULD CHOOSE		
A	**OR**	**B**
$681 billion Enough money to install the entire renewable energy infrastructure (page 167). 3000 TCP plants, 160,000 MW of fuel cells, 144,200 MW of solar electric, 215,00 MW of wind turbines and 34,000 MW of ocean turbines ...with $60 billion left over		**$681 billion** Bush tax cut dollars going only to the richest 1% over the seven years of the cut. These recipients are already millionaires.
$3 billion As a $50 per ton subsidy to **small** family farms to grow switchgrass, yellow mustard, soy or canola for biomass. It would be enough TCP feedstock to produce 5 billion gallons of fuel oil, half the transportation demand for the U.S. This subsidy would add $25,000 to 120,000 family farm incomes		**$3 billion** Subsidies to U.S. corporate cotton plantations, declared illegal by the world Trade Organization (WTO), have had the effect of lowering the world price of cotton by 40% driving 15 million small farming operations in Africa, Asia and Latin America into bankruptcy
106,600 Jobs Number of permanent, good paying jobs created in 133 counties that install a renewable energy infrastructure. In addition, over $18 billion would be put directly into the county economies		**106,600 Jobs** 25,700 Number of people fired from Hewlett-Packard in 2002 and replaced with outsourced help. Carla Fiorina, the CEO, was given a 230% raise to $4.1 million per year 20,000 Number of people fired from Merrill-Lynch in 2003. The CEO was rewarded with a salary increase from $14 million to $28 million per year 18,000 Number of people laid off by Boeing between September 2001 and September 2003. 42,900 Number of U.S. jobs eliminated by Motorola in 2001 while at the same time they invested $3.4 billion in China

IF YOU COULD CHOOSE

A OR	B
The abuses of the tax system listed on the right represent enough money to fund a total transition of the U.S. economy to renewable energy more than seven times over. Such a transition would create over six million jobs and put $300 billion into the U.S. economy every year	**$714 billion** Amount over ten years shifted to the wealthiest Americans with the Bush tax plan by eliminating taxes on corporate dividends. A New York Times ad, signed by 450 economists including 10 Nobel prize winners, claims that this giveaway will **harm** the U.S. economy
	$250 billion Annual loss to U.S. Treasury from corporations that use hidden tax entitlements and fake losses to avoid taxes
	$70 billion Annual lost revenue from off-shore corporate tax avoidance. HR-737 was proposed to stop this abuse but the legislation was prevented from coming to a vote by DeLay (R-TX) and Hastert (R-IN). Halliburton has 44 such offshore tax avoidance shelters. Enron had hundreds
	$50 billion Annual lost revenue from fraudulent tax loopholes exploited by individuals and marketed through accounting firms
*Read *Perfectly Legal*, Penguin Publications. New York (2003) by David Cay Johnston. The list on the right does not include the Bush income tax rebate which gives an additional $681 billion to the richest 1% -- people who are already millionaires. This alone would fund the transition to a renewable energy economy.	**$300 billion** Annual lost revenue from the Bush proposed elimination of the estate tax, which does not affect any family with an estate worth less than $7 million*
	$9.5 billion Cost to U.S. taxpayers for WorldCom (MCI) tax code manipulation

Too Costly And Impractical

We hear the criticism that while renewable energy may be a good idea, the technology is too costly and impractical to actually be put into place. So the logic goes, we have no choice but to continue pretty much the way we have been going with fossil fuel and nuclear energy...sorry, there is really no choice. This message is usually coming from someone who is directly associated with the fossil fuel/nuclear industries or is paid by them.

This chart can be used as a check to help you determine whether or not a strategy is indeed too costly and impractical Apply each of the 14 prompts to the strategy in question.

TOO COSTLY ?	IMPRACTICAL ?
Acquisition of Primary Energy	Engineering and Lifecycle Cost Considerations
Efficient use of Primary Energy, End Use Energy	The Chemistry and Physics
Clean up Costs - Who Pays?	Job Creation
Subsidies to Mature vs Emerging Industries	Effect on Local and State Economies
Military Involvement	Effect on U.S. Trade Deficit
The Grid	Effect on National Security
Externalities Who Pays?	Effect on Environment, Global Climate

We can use this chart to compare two strategies side by side.

For example compare nuclear to ocean turbines in the Gulf Stream. Which makes more sense? Which is the better idea in terms of being cost effective and practical?

For some people the nuclear strategy makes more sense, for some people, the ocean turbines would probably make more sense. Another question might be: for whose benefit is energy policy made?

TOO COSTLY ? N = Nuclear	IMPRACTICAL ? O= Ocean Turbines
Acquisition of Primary Energy N: Uranium ore must be mined; tailings must be stored in a safe place (not alongside the Colorado river). Ore must be purchased and processed O: It's free and readily accessible off the east coast of the U.S.	**Engineering and Lifecycle Cost Considerations** N: Theoretically the engineering is sound but engineering glitches are continuously cropping up and causing problems. Installed cost for nuclear is in the $3000 to $5000 per KW range O: Prototypes seem to work as designed; installed cost should be in the $1200 per KW range
Efficient use of Primary Energy, End Use Energy N: After about 3% of the energy is utilized, the other 97% becomes high-level nuclear waste O: No waste	**The Chemistry and Physics** N: Theoretically the science is sound. The problem is human negligence and incompetence O: There is tremendous kinetic energy in moving water, the turbine economically taps it, pretty straightforward
Clean up Costs N: It's a nightmare. In forty years no solution has been found for a repository. The costs are astronomical, estimated at $400 billion for the plants in the U.S. O: None	**Job Creation** N: Not known as a prolific job creator O: Most likely as good as nuclear in terms of job creation; jobs would be disbursed all up and down the east coast to maintain the turbines The manufacturing could be done anywhere in the U.S.
Subsidies to Mature vs Emerging Industries N: Nuclear has received over $200 billion in R&D and subsidies to date and are still receiving them after 40 years. The taxpayer must pay for their insurance O: Have not received any significant subsidies yet, can pay for their own insurance	**Effect on Local and State Economies** N: Minimal O: Certainly as much as nuclear
Military Involvement N: No, unless a power plant becomes a terrorist target. O: No	**Effect on U.S. Trade Deficit** N: Minimal O: Minimal
The Grid N: Required O: Required to some degree	**Affect on National Security** N: Nuclear plants are a proven security risk, spent nuclear material is also a big security risk. O: None
Externalities N: Adverse health effects associated with the mining and processing, decommissioning costs, insurance costs pushed onto the taxpayer O: None	**Effect on Environment, Global Climate** N: In terms of waste nuclear is a nightmare; in terms of climate change nuclear is not a viable strategy to lessen it, according to recent studies O: No negative impact on environment.

Compare a centralized coal fired power plant to SOFCs . Which makes more sense? Which is the better idea in terms of being cost effective and practical?

TOO COSTLY ?	IMPRACTICAL ?
C= Coal SOFC = Solid Oxide Fuel Cell	
Acquisition of Primary Energy C: Really cheap, $24 per ton, $1 per M-BTUs. Unless you include externalities into the fuel cost SOFC: Oil from the local TCP plant at $3 per M-BTUs, three times as much	**Engineering and Lifecycle Cost Considerations** C: Installed cost is in the $500-$600 per KW range, the technology is mature SOFC: Installed cost will come down to $400 per KW from the current $1200. No major engineering hurdles to overcome except getting the volume cost down further
Efficient use of Primary Energy, End Use Energy C: 34% plant efficiency, 66% lost as waste heat and internal losses SOFC: 92% overall efficiency with heat recovery	**The Chemistry and Physics** C: N/A, mature combustion technology SOFC: Fuel cell electrochemical technology. Will experience continued improvements as they are used more and more
Clean up Costs C: Mercury emissions end up in lakes, converted into methyl-mercury. Almost impossible to clean up SOFC: None	**Job Creation** C: Minimal as with all centralized technologies SOFC: Manufacturing on the state level would create hundreds of jobs, maintaining fuel cells on local level would create thousands of jobs
Subsidies to Mature vs Emerging Industries C: Continues to receive billions per year SOFC: Minimal. There is a small DOE program to develop SOFC technology	**Effect on Local and State Economies** C: Minimal, as with centralized technologies SOFC: The power generation is distributed as is the production of the fuel with TCP. The impact would be major
Military Involvement C: N/A SOFC: N/A	**Effect on U.S. Trade Deficit** C: Money goes out of state to purchase coal SOFC: Manufacturing the units, producing the fuel, maintaining the units is all locally done
The Grid C: The central plants are remote, often hundreds of miles from consumers, requires a grid SOFC: Distributed power eliminates the need for the grid	**Effect on National Security** C: N/A SOFC: N/A
Externalities C: Global climate change with carbon dioxide emissions, acid rain with sulfur and nitrogen oxide emissions, contributes to mercury caused neurological damage in 635,000 babies per year. SOFC: None	**Effect on Environment, Global Climate** C: Major effect, which corresponds to externalities because the cost for the damage is not borne by the utility. SOFC: None

Use the following two handy checklists to determine if an idea, a proposed energy strategy, is too costly or impractical.

A HANDY CHECKLIST ECONOMIC STRATEGIES FOR ACQUIRING LIQUID FUELS		
Item In Question	**Plan A**	**Plan B**
Proximity How far away from home is the primary resource? 10 miles, 40 miles? Farther than that? If further than 40 miles what is the reason for going so far?		
Jobs How many local jobs are created with this economic strategy?		
Local economies How much of the money used to purchase and process the primary resource stays local or within the state?		
Trade deficit Is the federal trade deficit affected?		
National security Does this strategy tend to make the U.S. safer or less safe?		
Environmental considerations What is the potential for spills in transport and production? How might sensitive environmental areas be affected? To what extent will waste products during use contaminate the air, land, oceans or fresh water? Is fossil carbon dumped into the atmosphere?		
Subsidies Who benefits from this strategy?		
Potential for corruption Whenever any resource with great value is controlled by a few who have garnered the political power to do so, there is the potential for corruption, undemocratic control of the wealth and repressive force. Might this be a problem for this economic strategy as it currently is for example in Uzbekistan, Chad-Cameroon, Saudi Arabia, Angola, Bolivia, Azerbaijan, Nigeria, Colombia, Burma, Indonesia Equatorial Guinea and Ecuador.		
Price instability, economic security How vulnerable is this strategy to outside forces, say terrorists who might like to cut off supplies or an organization of states such as OPEC that control the price.		
Cost Add up all of the costs: acquisition, transport, refining, spills, protection, etc.		
Military involvement Add up all of the costs, direct and indirect.		

A HANDY CHECKLIST
ECONOMIC STRATEGIES FOR PRODUCING ELECTRICITY

Item In Question	Plan A	Plan B
Legalities Problems in siting, locating the facility, opposition from locals: Is it costly and time consuming to deal with or are locals mostly in favor of the proposal and eager to have it in their community? Why are locals in opposition, are their fears justified or not?		
Engineering and construction How much lead-time is required, total time between OK and completion of project? Is design and construction by local entities or firms located afar?		
Manufacturing Is it modular, many units of the same size and configuration? Or is it large, complex, or singular "one off" custom design? Modularity gives flexibility in design as well as capacity and timing for future requirements. A one off, huge, complex plant means that much of the capacity sits idle before future requirements are needed. If future requirements are not needed then the capacity, money and effort is wasted.		
Funding Modular units can be funded easier and for less money for the same capacity.		
Installation What is the cost per installed KW?		
Operation and Maintenance How many good local jobs does this function support? What is worst case human error scenario?		
Transmission grid Is a grid required to get the electricity to the end users? What additional problems, opposition, security risks, expense and hazard does this entail?		
National security Is there radioactive material that must be controlled and kept out of the hands of terrorists? What is the industry record so far in being able to maintain security at similar facilities? What kind of target does the facility present to potential terrorists?		
The Mess What are the ongoing operational waste disposal concerns, have they traditionally been be met by this industry, what is the record? Who pays for decommissioning and what are the other realities regarding decommissioning? What are the environmental concerns?		
Safety What are the liability insurance requirements and who is expected to pay for the premiums? What are the implications of a serious operational failure and who pays?		
Politics Follow the money. Are there subsidies going to mature industries that are politically connected? Who benefits from this?		

CONCLUSION

So...if we have five times more energy than we need for a renewable energy economy, and ten times as much money as we need to fund it, and if we have the know-how with technologies all but ready to go....why don't we just do it? After all, there will be millions of new jobs created, thousands of revitalized communities across the country, the federal trade deficit will be cut in half, we will all be safer, and the environment will be saved.

As an economic strategy, it's a no brainer. With the old way, we pay out $750 billion per year; with the new way we not only do not have to pay the $750 billion, but we get $180 billion per year back. That's a $180 billion dollar per year positive cash flow. A $930 billion difference per year!

A renewable economy is decentralized with production and distribution at the local and county level; there is no need for huge regulatory and administrative federal bureaucracies. County TCP plants do not have to be regulated, SOFC electric does not have to be distributed on an international network, and there is no need for government agencies to administer the **LOCAL** production of energy.

In terms of political philosophy, it would seem hard to argue with the facts that there would be less government, less taxation, less government spending, a stronger national defense, less welfare to profitable corporations and a far greater opportunity for good old American "free market" economics to flourish. So, what's the problem?

The problem is that there are corporate entities that do not want to give up their current ability to turn a profit in an economic system that is based on the last remaining fossil fuels, whether it's oil, or central coal-fired power or 7,000 pound SUVs that profit the automaker at $15,000 per vehicle. The problem is that these corporate entities have political clout and play a big role in actually creating the energy policy of our country.

When this changes, we will be on our way to a renewable energy economy...and everyone will be better off, America, the global environment and future generations.

WHAT YOU CAN DO

The struggle to accomplish the transformation to a renewable energy based economy will be driven by ordinary people working within their communities.

•Educate yourself by using web sites such as H2FC.com (see list page 197) to learn about emerging renewable energy related technologies.

•Agitate. Write your local newspapers and call radio stations.

•Speak to groups, schools, Kiwanis, Lions, VFW, churches...any group that will have you. Use the overhead master and the talking point outline on the following three pages. These have been designed for your use and no permission is required to reproduce.

•Set up focus and discussion groups so interested people know they have support, resources and encouragement.

•Inventory the waste, biomass and wind resources in your county. Get a TCP or fast pyrolysis plant installed in your community.

•Take the message of this book to planners at the city, county and state levels and tell them how the renewable energy based economy benefits everyone...rejuvenated local economies, good jobs that cannot be outsourced and enhanced natural resources that result from a clean environment.

•Contact political candidates, at all levels. Remind them that funding renewable energy economic strategies is a political bonanza because renewable energy means local jobs and prosperity...and that means votes. There is a greater political advantage in representing ordinary people who want jobs than in being beholden to the fossil fuel and nuclear energy industries.

•Contact labor and business leaders and explain the benefits of adopting renewable energy in your community.

•If possible, purchase renewable energy and support renewable energy products.

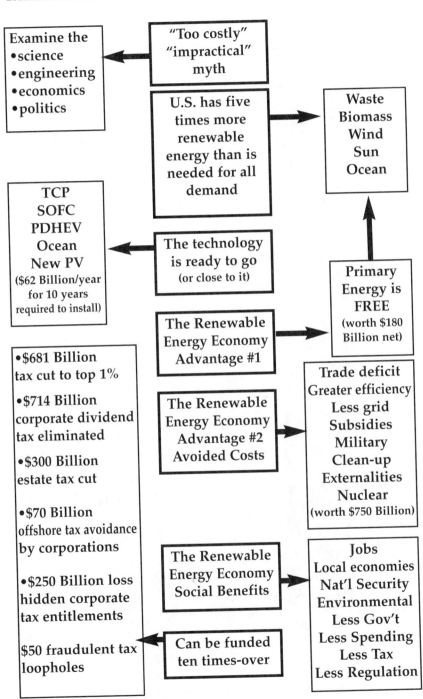

AVAILABLE U.S. RENEWABLE ENERGY

OTHER

GEO

SUN

WASTE BIO-MASS

WIND

RENEWABLE ENERGY

U.S. RENEWABLE ENERGY DEMAND

TRANS

HEAT

ELECTRICITY

AMOUNT OF AVAILABLE RENEWABLE ENERGY IN U.S.

AMOUNT OF RENEWABLE ENERGY NEEDED IN U.S.

$1240 BILLION

$310 BILLION+ LOST TO TAX SYSTEM ABUSE

FUNDING RENEWABLE ENERGY ECONOMY

IS THERE ENOUGH?

$180 BILLION NET VALUE ADDED

$750 BILLION AVOIDED COSTS

$62 BILLION PER YEAR FOR 10 YEARS

MONEY AVAILABLE TO FUND RENEWABLE ENERGY ECONOMY (20 TIMES AMOUNT NEEDED)

AMOUNT REQUIRED TO INSTALL RENEWABLE ENERGY ECONOMY

BIBLIOGRAPHY

American Chemical Society. *Chemistry in Context.* Second edition. WCB/McGraw Hill, 1997.

Ashworth, William. *The Economy of Nature, Rethinking the Connections between Ecology and Economics.* Boston: Houghton Mifflin, 1995.

Brower, Michael C. et al. *Powering the Midwest.* Union of Concerned Scientists, 1993.

Brower, Michael. *Cool Energy.* Cambridge: The MIT Press, 1994.

Caldicott, Helen. *If You Love This Planet: A Plan To Heal The Earth.* New York: W. W. Norton & Company, 1992

Chiras, Daniel D. *The Solar House.* White River Junction, VT: Chelsea Green Publishing, 2002.

Duffie, John A. and William A. Beckman. *Solar Energy Thermal Processes.* New York: John Wiley & Sons, 1974.

Hawken, Paul. *The Ecology of Commerce.* New York: Harper Collins, 1993.

Hoffmann, Peter. *Tomorrow's Energy.* Cambridge: MIT Press, 2002

Johnston, David Cay. *Perfectly Legal, The Covert Campaign to Rig Our Tax System To Benefit the Super Rich.* New York: Penquin, 2003.

Klass, Donald L. *Biomass for Renewable Energy, Fuels, and Chemicals.* London: Academic Press, 1998.

LaDuke, Winona. *All Our Relations, Native Struggles for Land and Life.* Cambridge: South End Press, 1999.

Lovins, Amory B. *Brittle Power, Energy Strategy for National Security.* Snowmass: Rocky Mountain Institute Press, 2001.

Lovins, Amory B. *Small is Profitable, the Hidden Economic Benefits of Making Electrical Resources the Right Size.* Snowmass: Rocky Mountain Institute Press, 2002.

Lovins, Amory B. *Soft Energy Paths: Toward a Durable Peace.* New York: Harper & Row, 1977.

Lovins, Amory B. *The Energy Controversy.* San Francisco: Friends of the Earth, 1979.

Mazria, Edward. *The Passive Solar Energy Book.* Emmaus, PA: Rodale Press, 1979.

Meadows, Donella H. *Beyond the Limits.* White River Junction, VT: Chelsea, 1992.

Nebel, Bernard J. and Richard T. Wright. *Environmental Science.* Seventh edition. Upper Saddle River, NJ: Prentice Hall, 2000.

Probstein, Ronald F. and R. Edwin Hicks. *Synthetic Fuels.* New York: McGraw-Hill, 1982.

Reece, Ray. *The Sun Betrayed, A Report on the Corporate Seizure of U.S. Solar Energy Development.* Boston: South End Press, 1979.

Rifkin, Jeremy. *The Hydrogen Economy.* New York: Putnam, 2002.

Schumacher, E. F. *Small is Beautiful, Economics as if People Mattered.* New York: Harper and Row, 1973.

Vaitheeswaran, Vijay V. *Power to the People.* New York: Farrar & Giroux, 2003.

Yergin, Daniel. *The Prize.* New York: Simon and Schuster, 1992.

Zepezauer, Mark and Arthur Naiman. *Take the Rich Off Welfare.* Tucson: Odonian Press, 1996.

INTERNET RESOURCES

Fuel Cells
astrisfuelcell.com
delphi.com
ftc.com
fuelcell.com
fce..com
hexis.com
nanodynamics.com
seca.doe.gov
sulzer.com

Solar
altairnano.com
hydrogensolar.com
iowathinfilm.com
seia.org
solaicx.com
shec-labs.com
spheralsolar.com
sunpowercorp.com
uni-solar.com

Wind
amec.com/wind
awea.com
dw-1.com
capewind.org
eren.doe.gov/wind
gepower.com
skywindpower.com
   (flying)
windustry.org
windpower.org
zilkha.com

PDHEV related
biodiesel.org
carbohydrateeconomy.com
dieselforum.org.
electricdrive.org
greasecar.com
greasel.com
hydradix.com (H_2 reformer)
methanol.org
ncaur.usda.gov (biofuel)
qtww.com (H_2 storage)
theaircar.com
uqm.com
veggievan.org
wavecrestlabs.com

Policy
costofwar.com
iags.org
essentialinformation.org
   (corporate tax abuse)
faireconomy.org
fairtaxes4all.org
ilsr.org
nuclearpolicy.org
pirg.org
prwatch.org
repowermidwest.org
rmi.org
sustainableenergy.org
   (Bush environmental score)
tompaine.com
uscaction.org (USC)
worldpolicy.org

Miscellaneous
alchemix.net
changingworldtech.com
   (TCP)
dynamotive.com
eia.doe.gov
   (energy statistics)
geo-energy.org
   (geothermal)
h2fc.com
iaus.com
   (propulsion turbine)
oceanpd.com (wave)
oceanpowertechnologies.
   com
re-focus.com
verdantpower.com
   (ocean)
wavedragon.net

OIL TERMINOLOGY

Biodiesel a renewable oil product made by chemically altering naturally occurring oils and fats, usually from soybeans or canola.

Biofuel fuels that are derived from living or recently living plant matter, including biodiesel, biogas, gasahol, bio-oil and TCP oil.

Biogas methane and carbon dioxide mixture resulting from the anaerobic digestion of agricultural waste, sewage, manure or biomasss.

Bio-oil a highly oxygenated, renewable oil product produced by the fast pyrolysis process having 55% of the volumetric energy of petroleum diesel, but with no sulfur and less nitrous oxide content.

Carbon Neutral the cycling of carbon in energy conversion systems, where the net amount of carbon in the ecosystem remains relatively constant. Even though carbon dioxide is released in the combustion of wood, for example, it is reabsorbed in a short time by the living, growing plants. This is in contrast to extracting carbon from the ground where it has been for millions of years and dumping the products from its combustion into the atmosphere (as carbon dioxide) where it accumulates over time resulting in a net increase in carbon in the atmosphere.

Fossil fuel coal, crude oil and natural gas. Referred to as fossil fuels because they were formed from living organisms that have undergone heat and compression underground over a period of hundreds of millions of years.

Hydrocarbons chemical compounds composed of carbon and hydrogen atoms.

Liquified natural gas (LNG) natural gas, primarily methane, that is stored and transported as a liquid but requires high pressure as well as low temperatures (-117°F or -83°C). Natural gas can be shipped in bulk as LNG using highly insulated tankers and requiring special port facilities for unloading.

Liquified petroleum gas (LPG) various mixtures of natural gas, primarily propane and butane, that can be stored as a liquid under pressure at ambient temperatures.

Natural gas a gaseous fossil fuel, often found in conjunction with crude oil, consisting chiefly of methane (85%), ethane (up to about 10%) propane (about 3%) and some butane.

Non-renewable energy sources of energy that are acquired (mined), used and the waste products dumped into the ecosystem. Fossil fuels and fission fuels (uranium ore) are examples of non-renewable energy sources.

Petroleum a naturally occurring liquid fossil fuel composed of a complex mixture of hydrocarbons. Also referred to as crude oil in its unrefined form. Crude oil is a non-renewable resource since it has been in place for millions of years and cannot be renewed.

> **Crude oil** is refined by fractional distillation into refinery gas (methane, ethane, butane and propane), gasoline, kerosene and diesel oil.
>
> **Gasoline** a mixture of hydrocarbons containing 5-8 carbon atoms.
>
> **Kerosene** a mixture of hydrocarbons containing 11-12 carbon atoms and used as jet fuel.
>
> **Diesel oil** a mixture of hydrocarbons containing 13-25 carbon atoms, light diesel oil is also called #2 fuel oil, a common heating fuel.

Renewable Energy sources of energy that continue to recycle within the eco-system. Energy contained in the carbon-hydrogen and carbon-oxygen chemical bonds is released under certain conditions such as combustion and stored under certain conditions such as photosynthesis. The ultimate source of the energy is radiation from the sun. Examples of renewable energy include wind, ocean waves and currents and biomass.

TCP oil a light fuel oil comparable to diesel derived from renewable feedstock sources such as garbage, plastics, used tires, agricultural waste and biomass by depolymerizing the feedstock under high pressure and temperature and reforming the mixture into oil and other by-products.

INDEX

Aceh 116
Acid rain 95,100,118,187
Activated carbon 134,158,159
Adding Value to Waste 158
Agricultural Crop 17,135
Air Products, Inc.
Alaska 90,117,119,178,179
Alcohol Solutions LLC 192
Alkaline 27
Alkaline zinc/matrix 127
AMEC Project Investments Ltd. 142
American Gas Association 169
Anaerobic digestion 169
Anode catalyst 33
Anthrax 17
Appel, Brian 19, 150
Arctic National Wildlife Reserve
   (ANWR) 149
Audi A2 24
Bandar, Prince 119
Battery Technology 26-27,127
Benzene 120
Biocatalysis 59
Biomass gasification 58
Bird kills 48
Black liquor gasification 56
Black Lung 95,96
Boeing 181, 183
Bookman, Jay 115
Bovine spongeform encephalopathy
   20, 173
Brown algae 169
Bunker oil 95,118
Bush 90,97,103,107,108,110,111,
   113,115,116,178,180,183,184
California, Hayward 44
Cahill, Thomas 88
Californians for Alternatives to
   Toxics 45
Caño Limon pipeline 178
Capital and Income 83
Carbohydrate 29,65,66

Carbon black 17, 19, 158-159, 165,
   173
Carbon dioxide 25,65,66,68,88,89,
   97,100 120,153,167,187
Carbon neutral 20, 25, 82,171,198
Carthage, Missouri 18, 173
Caspian 114,115
Cathode 26, 33
Cellulosic biomass 19, 59, 134
Changing World Technologies 17-19
Chatterjee, Pratap 115
Chicago 121,178
Clipper Windpower 29,49
Coal
32,39,74,75,82,94,95,96,99,103,
   147,148,150,153,157,180,187,190
   Black Lung 95,96
   Mercury in the coal 98
   Mine Reclamation 95,99
   Mining the Coal 94, 95
   Pollution from coal plants 95,99
   Respiratory Disease 95,99
   Subsidies 103
   Transporting the Coal 95,97
Coast Guard 178
Colombia 117,122,178,188
Combined cycle 34, 39,158,159
Combustion 25,33, 36, 65, 68,98,
   153,187
Commission on Radiological
   Protection 105
Commons 61,85
Conservation and Efficiency
   29,76,77
Cows 173
Crowell, Aaron 171
Davis-Besse 106,111
Decommissioning 87,95,109,110,
   113,180,186,189
DeLay 184
Denmark 49,51,157,160
Department of Energy 49,90,104,
   107,142,143,159,169,179

Department of the Navy 169
Dimethyl ether (DME) 136
Dioxin 17
Direct Methanol Fuel Cells (DMFC) 64,35,37
Discover Magazine 16
Distributed generation 37,43,50, 77,78,98,129,134,145
Dominion Energy 107,181
Downer cows 173
DuPont Corporation 41
Dye sensitized solar cells 43,45
DynaMotive Corp. 60
Eastman Kodak Corporation 57
Electrolysis 30,65,67
Electrolyzer 30-31
Embedded electric motor 22
Enclosure 85
Energy crops 135
Energy demand 12,128,144,181
Energy, cost of 75,87,103,154,157
Engineering Business 52
Enron 184
Entergy 107,181
Enzymes 59
Ecuador 123,188
Ethylene 58
Ethylene synthesis 58
European Committee of Radiation Risk 105
European Union 105,157
Exelon Corp 181
Exothermic 34
Exponential growth 83,84
Externalities 61,78,79,86,87,93,94, 96,113,122,123,134,147,151,157, 163,168,176,185,186,187
Exxon 82,103,114,115,116,119,182
Fast pyrolysis 17,56,60,134,136,149, 150,153,181,192,198
Feedlot manure 17,135
Fiat 25
Fisher-Tropsch 134

Flaring 95,114,117,120
Flat plate solar collector 40
Florida Hydro Power & Light 72
Flying wind generator 50
Forbes 106,109
Forestry waste 17-18,135
Fuel Cell Energy 36, 153, 155
Fuel cell energy flow 153, 155
Fuel cells 21,27,28,30,32,33,34,36, 37,38,64,77,113,128,129,136,145,1 50,152,153,154,159,160,162,165,1 77,178,179,183,187
    Direct Methanol Fuel Cells (DMFC) 64,35,37
    High Temperature Fuel Cells 32,34,77,113,152,153,160,165, 177,178,179
    Microbial Fuel Cells 38
    Proton Exchange Membrane (PEM) 33-34
    Solid Oxide Fuel Cells (SOFC) 13,21,30,36,37,39,64,145,158, 159,161,164,165,181,187
Gas Research Institute 169
Gas to liquid processes 59, 134
Gasoline 23,24,25,28,54,55,56,64, 75,80,113,120,123,126,127,136, 145,170,177
General Motors (GM) 22,23
Geothermal 73,142,143,145
Global Energy Concepts 49
Global warming basics 88
Global warming87,88,90,91,94,95, 96,97,101,102,103,118,120,157, 163,168
Graeve, Phil 171
Ground Mounted Solar (GS) 40-41
Ground Mounted Solar/ Refrigerant Turbine (GSRT) 13,46,64,165,166,167,182
Gulf Stream 15,53,72,165,185
Gustavus Adolphus College 171
Halliburton 115,177,184

Hastert 184
Haudenosaunee teaching 82
High Temperature Fuel Cells
    32,34,77,113,152,153,160,165,
    177,178,179
House of Representatives . 180
House of Saud 172
HR-737 184
Human Rights Watch 115
Hummer 29, 180
Hydraulic drive wheel 21
Hydraulic drive train 26
Hydraulic hybrid SUV 26
Hydrogen 64
    energy carrier 64
    hydrogen by volume 80
    hydrogen by weight 35-36
    hydrogen chemical bonds 67
    hydrogen economy 30,64,79,197
    Hydrogen fuel cell 20, 69
    Hydrogen fuel cell vehicle 30,31
    hydrogen gas 30,31,33,34,36,80
    Hydrogen physics 79
    Problems with hydrogen 55
Indonesia 116,188
Inhoffe, Senator James 163
Insurance Industry 91,101,163
International Labor Rights Fund 116
Johnston, David Cay 184
Journal of Environmental
    Epidemiology and Toxicology 105
JP-8 56,120,121
Karimov, Islam 115
Kelp 169
Klass, Donald L. 169
La Hague 105
Landfill gas 64
Lead-acid 27
League of Conservation Voters 112
Leasing arrangements 157
Limited Liability Corporations
    (LLCs) 111
Linear 81,82,83,84,88

Liquid phase conversion 57
Lithium chemistries 26
Lithium-ion 26-27
Lithium-polymer 27, 127
Lithium-sulfur 27, 127
Locomotive 20Loker
Hydrocarbon Research
    Institute 58
Loux, Robert 110
Lovins, Amory 43,98,108
Macrocystis pyrifera 169
Mad cow 20, 173
Marine Current Turbines 52
Medis Technologies 35
Mendeleev, Dimitri 54
Mercury 86,94, 95,98,168,187
Methanol 35,36,56,57,58,63,64,75,
    120,134,136,153
Methanol Institute 57
Methanol Synthesis 56, 134
Microbial Fuel Cells 38
Moab 104
Municipal Sewage 135
Municipal Solid Waste 17,135,151,159
Mutagenic 56
National Renewable Energy
    Laboratory (NREL)48,177
NiCad 27
NiMetal Hydride 27
Nigeria 116,117,120,188
Nitrogen reformers 25,
Nitrous oxides 100, 101,70
Northern Power Systems 49
Nuclear 95,103
Nuclear Power Plant 106
    Uranium ore 62,95,104,186
Nuclear industry 55,87,95,105,
    107,108,109,111,112,113,179,180,
    181
Nuclear Material 87,95,186
Occidental Petroleum 122,178
Ocean Systems 16,51,133,142,145
Oil pipelines 114,117
Olah, Dr. George 58

OPEC 119,134,188
Opel-ECO 24
Operational Safeguards
  Response Evaluation 109
OPIC 95,117,180
Ozone 101
Passive Solar 13,41,42,127,145,
  164,165,167,196
PDHEV 13,16,20-22,26,28-32,127,
  129,137, 165,166, 167, 169, 177, 180
Pelamis 51
Pentagon 90,114,121,163,177,178
Perfectly Legal 184
Photosynthesis 45,65,66
Photovoltaics (PV) 13,43-46, 73,
  129,140,141,144,145,164,166,179
Plastics 17-18,46,135
Plug In Diesel Hybrid Electric
  Vehicle see PDHEV
Prestige 118,119
Price-Anderson 95,112,177
Probstein, Ronald F. 58
Production Tax Credit 49,157,180,
  181
Proton Exchange Membrane
  (PEM) 33-34
Prueitt, Dr. Mel 40
Pulp industry 57
Pusan University 46
PVC (polyvinyl chloride) 17
Pyrolysis 17
Queen Mary-2 20
Radiant energy 141
Raymond, Lee 82
Regenerative braking 21,23,30,
  31,127
Regenerative particulate filters 25
Restaurant Grease 24,135,168,
  170,171
Rhodes, Cecil 85
Rhodoferax ferrireducens 38
Rocky Mountain Institute 43,77,
  98,196

Royal Dutch Shell Oil Company
  29,90
Rumsfeld, Donald 115
San Francisco Board of
  Supervisors 53
Saudi Arabia 118,119,188
Seaweed 168,169
Sellafield 105
Senate Appropriations Committee 179
Senate bill-14 181
Shipping 53,118,119
Silicon 43
    Crystalline Silicon 43,44,45
    Thin Film Amorphous Silicon 44
SOFC see fuel cells
Solar Energy Limited 41
Solar Thermal 13,40,41,73,127,
  128,145,164,165,167,178
Solawatt 40
Solid Oxide Fuel Cells see fuel cells
South Africa 58
Starch 59
Steam Turbine 34, 159
Stevens, Ted 179
Stingray 52
Straight vegetable oil 170
Stranded costs 112
Subsidies ,57,94,103,111,113,121,
  122,123,147,168,176,177,179,180,
  183,185,186,187,188,189
Sudan 116
Sulfur 20,25,27,65,97,100,118,120,
  127,170,187
Sustainability 61,81,83,86,
Sustainable growth 83
Sweden 100
Switchgrass 135, 183
Syn-gas 17
Tar Sands 135
Taylor, Trey 53
TC process 17-19,21,36,134,137,
  149, 151, 159
Tefzel 41

Terrorism 95,108,110,114,117,119
Thermal depolymerization 136,149
Tires 17,134,135,151,159
Toluene 56
Trade deficit 15,20,28,147,163 167, 168,174,176,177,185,186,187,188, 190
Transmission Lines 70,95,98,138
Turbocharged direct injection (TDI) 25
U.S. Public Interest Research Group (USPIRG) 111
U.S. treasury 122,180,184
Underwater turbines 52,53
Union of Concerned Scientists 48, 70,107,109,111,138
Uni-Solar 44
University of Arizona 46
University of California (Berkeley) 46
UQM Technologies 22-23
Variable valve actuation 25
Verdant Power 52,53
Volumetric Energy Content 30,64, 75,76,79,80,134,170
VW Caddy 24
VW Jetta 24
VW Polo 24
Washington 103,115,176,181
Waste and Biomass Resources 135, 36,145
Water Chemistries 26
Wave systems 51
Wavecrest Laboratories 22-23
Wavedragon51
Weapons of mass destruction 178
Wind 136
    Offshore wind 142,143,145
    Wind energy 49,50,70,71,136, 138140,143,145,156,157,165, 172,177,179,181

Wind continued
    Wind resources 70,138,145
    Wind generators 47,48,49,53, 70,71,136,138,140,172
Wisbrock, William 57
World Bank 103,115,117
WorldCom 184
Yamaha Motors 35
Yucca Mountain 108,110
Zeolite catalyst 58
Zero Energy Homes 127
Zinc matrix 26-27
Zogby, John 179